Thomas Hunter

Reflections Critical and Moral on the Letters of the Late Earl of Chesterfield

Thomas Hunter

Reflections Critical and Moral on the Letters of the Late Earl of Chesterfield

ISBN/EAN: 9783337018757

Printed in Europe, USA, Canada, Australia, Japan

Cover: Foto ©ninafisch / pixelio.de

More available books at **www.hansebooks.com**

REFLECTIONS
CRITICAL AND MORAL
ON THE
LETTERS
OF THE LATE
EARL OF CHESTERFIELD.

By THOMAS HUNTER, M.A.
Vicar of Weaverham in Cheshire.

Great men are not always wise: neither do the aged understand judgment.
                                    Job xxxii. 9.

Si la noblesse est vertu, elle se perd par tout ce qui n'est pas verteux; et si elle n'est pas vertu c'est peu de chose.
                                    M. de la Bruyere.

THE SECOND EDITION.

LONDON:
Printed for T. CADELL, Bookseller in the Strand.
MDCCLXXVII.

TO THE
RIGHT REVEREND FATHER IN GOD

WILLIAM,

Lord Biſhop of CHESTER,

DEAN OF CHRIST CHURCH,

AND PRECEPTOR TO THEIR ROYAL HIGHNESSES

GEORGE PRINCE OF WALES,

AND

FREDERICK BISHOP OF OSNABRUG.

MY LORD,

ONE who cenſures ſo popular and cele-brated a writer as the Lord CHESTERFIELD, hath need of all honeſt advanta-

A 2   ges,

ges, to avoid the prejudices, to bespeak the attention, and engage the favour and candour of the public. The author of these sheets pretends to no advantages but such as a regard to truth, to virtue and the happiness of mankind may give him. He, therefore, calls on your Lordship as his patron and protector, to give him countenance, and to introduce him with credit into the world upon this occasion.

DEDICATION. v

sion. Your Lordship's name is great : and, the high offices, to which, without the arts of faction or the efforts of ambition, you have been called, — of a Christian Prelate and a Preceptor to Princes, may be thought to have some weight in the balance against titled greatness and patrician splendor.

But, abstracting from all titular distinction and external

external grandeur, which constitute no part of the great or moral man; should we contrast with the splendid portrait of perfection which Lord Chesterfield affects to give us in his own conduct, and in the lessons which he prescribes to his son, a character of a different form and feature, it would for ever discredit the cause of false politeness, and the principles

ples and practises of its insidious advocate.

The great and good man depends on truth and nature, not on artifice and fallacy, for his success. He is single in his views, his words and actions. He is what he seems: he speaks what he thinks: he intends what he professes: he is faithful to his word as to his oath. He scorns alike simulation and dissimulation,

on, under whatever specious sophistry distinguished or recommended. He is eminent for native strong sense, improved and adorned, not only by a just taste for polite letters, and elegant composition, but, by useful and extensive science. He listens more to the dictates of reason, than to the arts of refinement, and dwells more on the general rule than on the exception. He is equally unaffected

in

in his manners and style. He is serious, manly, firm and elevated; steady and inflexible in the prosecution of truth and justice; and, amidst the various and fluctuating notions of nominal and latitudinarian Christians, an undissembled assertor of the faith once delivered to the Saints.

When we observe prudence renouncing craft, wisdom

wisdom not debased by intrigue, sagacity and success not disgraced by artifice and hypocrisy: When eminence appears without magnificence, elevation without pride, superiority without vanity, and significance and importance of character without the parade of outward eclat, and the badges of office and honour: When the man, the citizen, the Briton appears distinguished by fidelity

delity to his friends, by compaffion to the miferable, by relief to the oppreffed, by favour to the good, by protection to the learned, by love to his country, and loyalty to his prince, upon principles of confcience and conviction: When an undiffembled zeal for GOD and his truth, as the foundations on which the pillars of the moral and civil world are fupported, form the ruling passion of the heart, and give law to the general conduct: When we view such a character, we look down with contempt on those superficial graces, to the study and attainment of which Lord Chesterfield would be thought to confine all the business of education, and all the perfection of human nature.

But, my Lord, I dare not proceed. Your Lordship

ship does not seek, as you do not want the applause of man. Besides, we have found, by experience, that a great and illustrious character has, sometimes, suffered by the display, and been regarded, if not resented as a libel upon the bulk of mankind : like a body eminently luminous, which affords not pleasure, but offence and pain to a weak and distempered eye. I will not, therefore, by attempting a full and more perfect portrait of your Lordship, hurt the pride, mortify the ignorance, and provoke the envy and malignity of the vulgar-spirited reader; and shall content myself with wishing, that such characters as your Lordship's may never be wanting to confront the vain wit, the false philosopher, the dissembling politician, the ignoble

noble patrician, and the profligate man of pleaſure.

The beſt title which theſe Reflections have to your Lordſhip's patronage is, that they are meant to co-operate with your Lordſhip's example, which holds out to us ſo different a ſtyle and order of perfection to that adopted and recommended by the noble Lord; as the exemplary lives of Chriſtians, in general, and of the Christian Clergy, in particular, will always be the best recommendation of their religion, and the most effectual confutation of those who deny its influence and authority by their practice or opinions.

I am,

MY LORD,

Your Lordship's
most dutiful
and devoted Servant,

THOMAS HUNTER.

PREFACE.

WE are sometimes overtaken by dead calms, and, sometimes assaulted by ruder tempests in the voyage of life, which damp the vigour and activity of the soul, and render us alike incapable of discharging the ordinary offices, and of sharing in the innocent pleasures of our being. In either case, our care, next to that of devoting and, resigning ourselves to the great

great pilot of nature, will be to amuſe, as well as we can, and to fill up the vacant hours with what may be agreeable to ourſelves, though not profitable to others. But, if we can render our amuſements of any advantage to the world, we have the comfort of reflecting, that we are not uſeleſs members of ſociety; that we do not live in vain, and, that an incapacity for greater atchievements may have its uſe in the plan of Providence, by ſuggeſting a ſtricter attention to the humbler offices of life.

We may not be qualified to conduct

PREFACE.

conduct armies, to fight battles, to extend empire abroad, or to defend and secure its liberties at home; we may not presume to inform princes, or to teach senators wisdom. But if we have, still, any ability left to instruct the ignorant, to direct the wanderer, to reclaim the flagitious, to support the weak, to confirm the virtuous, to remove prejudices, to vindicate, or in any degree to promote the virtue and happiness of mankind;---we acknowledge, we adore the hand of Heaven in our situation.

LORD CHESTERFIELD's Letters were

were firſt taken up as an amuſement to deceive the paſſing moments. They were, indeed, amuſing, but ſoon appeared alarming. The reader found his faith, his virtue, his underſtanding inſulted; and the ſentiments of the juſt and good in all ages and nations of the world who were favoured with almoſt any degree of light, of truth and ſcience oppoſed and contradicted, by our well-bred and courtly philoſopher. The mere reader was thus led to commence author; and, very freely to expreſs his indignation and contempt of a writer, who, great and

PREFACE.

and shining as his abilities were, hath disgraced, by applying them, to poison the morals, to banish the sublimest virtue, to extinguish the most salutary truths, and to exterminate the most important interests and the sincerest happiness of mankind.

If the author of these sheets has made his amusements, any way, contribute to the benefit of others, by exposing this seductive and dangerous writer; he will be abundantly satisfied with the consciousness of having discharged his duty; regardless of the reproach he may incur, for

for presuming to censure so popular, so polite, so distinguished a nobleman.

The subject of enquiry is truth and virtue. Here, therefore, we affect no complaisance or servility; our reflections are the dictates of the heart. Lord Chesterfield is regarded and addressed not as a nobleman, but as a man, a moralist and a citizen; and God alone is appealed to, as the judge of all.

ERRATA.

Page 47, line 4, for *humane* read *human*.
    59,   2, for *hear* read *here*.
    61,   antepenult. for *lead* read *led*.
  139,   9, for *cunduct* read *conduct*.
  146, Note, antepenult. for *fans* read *sans*.
  192, line 7, for *affects* read *effects*.
  210,   6, for *fortune* read *torture*.
  222,   13, for *extience* read *existence*.

REFLECTIONS
CRITICAL AND MORAL
ON THE
LETTERS
OF THE LATE
EARL OF CHESTERFIELD.

SECT. I.

TO censure is a disagreeable part to the candid writer, and reader: To censure, where great and conspicuous merit is allowed, wears the appearance of still more malignity:

SECTION I.

malignity: But, to cenfure a Writer fo generally celebrated and admired as the Lord Chefterfield, muft prove ftill more offenfive and perhaps more dangerous to the reputation of the critic, than of the author whom he affects to condemn.

But there is a ftrength and beauty in truth and virtue, a power and authority in religion which carry us beyond ourfelves, and difpofe us to a contempt of danger and difficulty, in their fupport and defence: Thofe principles were of little value, which are not worth defending at the hazard of our being. Dear as reputation, and awful as the reproach of the world may be to an author, an honeft man will prefer the difcharge of his duty, and the approbation of his confcience

SECTION I.

science and his GOD, to the united applause of the universe.

YET a regard to truth will preclude unjust prejudice, as well as general reprobation; and to deny a writer the praise to which he has a claim, on account of the censure to which he is liable, were no less impolitic than unjust. Let us, therefore, do justice to Lord Chesterfield as a Writer, before we proceed to condemn him as an Author.

To do justice to Lord Chesterfield's composition would require a pen like his own: Or let his Lordship's favourites, Venus and the Graces, join in concert to sing his eulogium!

WE should not do him sufficient justice,

justice, should we only say that he is clear and easy, natural and unaffected: for he is figurative, florid, ornamented and highly polished. He does not hurt the ear, encumber the sense, or perplex our thoughts with long and tedious sentences; but is, every where, pure; short, but expressive; concise, but not abrupt; full and satisfactory, but not voluminous; and has generally united laconic brevity with attic elegance. He is happy in expressions always suited to his subject; and nothing is farther from affectation than his language. I presume, he was accustomed to speak with the same ease and propriety that he writes. It seems natural to him: or, art had assumed so just a cast, and so well imitated the tone of nature, that we cannot distinguish the one from the other.

LORD

SECTION I. 5

Lord Chesterfield's style is music, filling and delighting the ear with the most melting notes, and the sweetest and most happy cadences: or, his hand may be said to be that of one of the first masters in painting, who presents you with the gayest scenery, the loveliest landscapes, and the most splendid colouring in nature. A brook, however pure and transparent, is too diminutive an object to give us a just resemblance of the Lord Chesterfield's style and manner. We may compare his Lordship's composition to a stream (were not this, likewise, too trite an image) full, but not redundant; loud, but not noisy; smooth and placid, yet not languid or sluggish; strong, but not harsh, dissonant or raging; harmonious in its course, musical in its falls; and, in the whole, feasting the eye, the ear, the fancy, the sensitive taste, and all the animal faculties and passions of the man. Its banks are crowned with all the beauties of simple nature; or with ornaments formed after the models, or answering to our ideas, of perfect nature. We have only to lament, that the source from whence it flows is tainted, and conveys a subtle poison, fatal to the lives of those who indulge, at large, in the tempting stream.

In his moral lessons, he gives us not only the trite apothegm, or thread-bare maxim; but he illustrates his observations by happy allusions, enlivens them by wit, enforces them by reason, and recommends them by proper examples; so that you are not only

SECTION I.

only instructed, but pleased, not, merely, informed, but charmed with his manner, his language and address: with much simplicity he has much purity; and, is, at the same time, both easy and elegant.

He seems to be always calm, recollected and in good humour; happy in an uniform tranquillity, the effect of natural temper and gaiety of heart; and these cherished and improved by cultivation, by polite letters, and by that ease and serenity, that indolence, that independence which every friend of the Muses ought, or would be thought, to be possessed of. His fortune, his titles and honours might be assigned as contributing to this happy spirit, did we not observe men possessed of all these, not distinguished by their humanity, their placability, or good temper.

He is not so laboured and affectedly learned as Lord Bolingbroke; but, then, he is more clear, more easy and agreeable; and insults not his readers with such a profusion of erudition, and such an exhibition of superior reasoning, upon every subject that occurs, as tend to speak him supreme dictator, in letters as in politics, in theology as in philosophy, and, next to the infinite Creator, the first genius in the universe. Lord Chesterfield is, in his writings, what, we presume, he was, in his life;—humane, chearful, complaisant and obliging; entertaining without form, and instructive without pride or insolence; desirous, at the same time, to please and to inform;

SECTION I.

inform; and aiming to advise as a friend, rather than to dictate as a master.

He has a quick and clear conception on the subjects that lie within his sphere,—a fine imagination, an accurate and just taste for composition and works of genius, with a peculiar beauty of expression; the allusions he, oftentimes, makes use of, have not, only, a perfect propriety, but a singular delicacy and poetical justness, in their application. He has not, indeed, given us much that is new, on the subject of criticism; but his own composition and letters exhibit the justest specimen of that correctness, perspicuity and elegance, which he recommended to the practice of his son: and, a thousand critical precepts

would

would not contribute, so much, to form a perfect style, as his own example.

His wit is prompt and natural, yet keen and manly: and volumes could scarce contain a stronger satyr against pedants and antiquarians, than what is couched in one short sentence, amongst the directions for his son's studies: " Let blockheads read what blockheads write."

It is much to the honour of Lord Chesterfield, that, amidst dissipation and pleasure, the offices and honours which he supported, as a Senator and a Statesman, favoured by fortune and flattered by the popular voice, he still preserved a good general reputation, leisure for study and taste for polite letters.

SECTION I.

letters. He appears to have had a real love of knowledge, and to have made such a proficiency in literature, both ancient and modern, as do distinguished credit to his title and character in life; and the cloistered sage, with all the opportunities and advantages of studious retreat, may blush at his own indolence and ignorance, when compared with the activity exercised, and the range taken, by this enterprizing genius.

His acquaintance with books was, indeed, uncommon for a man of quality; as his taste and judgment were more just and solid than might be expected from a man of fashion; who, in forming the character and directing the conduct of his son, recommends to him, and prefers, shew to substance, and splendour to weight.

As a critic, his lordship, in conformity to the best modern authors, both French and English, adopts simplicity and truth, before affectation, conceit, refinement, and brilliancy: and though, we say, he has given us nothing new or original, on this subject, yet we cannot but regard the Lord Chesterfield's verdict as valuable, and his comment as judicious in favour of truth, simplicity and the genuine beauties of nature.

He has not only a just but a refined taste, in the polite arts and polite letters. He joins the general approbation and applause given to the great masters

SECTION I.

masters of antiquity; (except in the case of Homer; the natural, the genuine, and rude manners of whose heroes hurt the delicacy of our modern man of fashion). He does justice to their general characters, and sometimes aptly, points out their particular beauties. He, acutely, exposes the affected pedant, the scholar without taste, and the virtuoso without sentiment. He was a more equal judge of the ancients, than of the moderns: in his report and character of these last, he was prejudiced by friendship, by passion, by his morals, and by the political maxims which concur with and favour his own.

His imagination was lively, and his memory strong. The traces which his favourite objects, a fine sentiment

SECTION I.

in an author, or a quick fenfation of pleafure had made upon him, feem to have retained their colour, flavour and impreffion upon his fancy, to extreme old age: and, he is happy, enough, in recollecting and applying the ideas he had ftored up, in the courfe of his former polite converfation and reading. Amidft diffipation, pleafure and bufinefs, he poffeffed a very clear and cool head; and may feem to have ftudied his fubjects on good manners and the world, as he has treated them, with all the precifion, attention and accuracy of a profeffor.

YET difpaffionate as he feems, he was no reafoner. Wit, which was his talent, is ftruck, and expects others fhould be fo, with the prefent thought, without regarding confiftency, or purfuing

SECTION I. 15

suing consequences. He has himself practised the maxims which he has given his son, and aims more to gain the passions than to convince the understanding of his readers.

EASY in his fortune, content with his reputation, satisfied with his rank and station, and finding, or imagining, himself at liberty to indulge to pleasure, to gay amusements and polite studies, it does not appear that he had been in any signal distress, or acquainted with any weight of sorrow, or calamity in life. Thus discharged from the discipline of the severer virtues, he had the greater range for imagination and pleasure, and was conversant and familiar with ideas the most gay and festive in nature. A stranger to the wants, the drudgery and

and business of life, he gave full play to his genius and constitution; to wit, to frolic, to delicacy, to the taste and fashion of the world; and mistakes pleasure for happiness, pomp for greatness, splendour for glory, and popular estimation for real good fame. Thus disposed, he devoted, he sacrificed himself to the Graces, and to the attainment of such qualities and accomplishments as were best fitted to please, to attract, and raise the admiration of mankind, and to gratify his own vanity and selfishness. Hence, he who considered this world as his all, was lead to deal, as much as possible, in the pleasurable, the brilliant, the shewy and pompous tracts of life; to study pleasure as a science; and to practise it as others do the ordinary occupations of life. His heart, his head,

SECTION I. 17

head, the whole man was infected with this enchanting sorceress. His style in writing naturally contracted a cast and colour from his habit of thinking and acting: and from the man of pleasure, of taste and elegance, we expect, what we find, in Lord Chesterfield, ideas, and a diction gay, refined and elegant. His lyre answered to the pulse of his heart, and the enchantress pleasure attunes the notes, and harmonizes the periods of his composition. With delight we listen to the syren song, though we reject the subject and matter with scorn, contempt and indignation.

He took, and advised his friend to take the gentle, the favourable, the indulgent side of most questions, and consequently avoided as much as possible all occasion of disquiet and disgust.

This world was his paradife; and he made the moft of it. This defpicable clod, this wildernefs, barren and imperfect as it is, affords many a fertile fpot, refrefhing ftream, happy fhade and delightful profpect: he obferved, he collected, he enjoyed them; and if, from thence, he contracted no moral, no manly, no rational, or religious joy and complacency; yet, he derived from them a natural, a fenfitive and animal pleafure; which fupported and recruited his fpirits, and enlarged and enlivened his imagination.

A COMPOSED and happy temper, a heart at eafe, and an independent fituation, are perhaps the moft favourable circumftances in an author's fortune. Traduced by the envious and malignant, hated by the rich, fufpected ed by the proud, and overlooked by the great, forgotten or coldly respected by his friends, and only noticed by his enemies, he has neither genius to project, nor spirit to prosecute any bold or extensive scheme of literature. Lord Chesterfield was free from all incumbrances of this sort, which might damp his spirit, or confine his genius. Raised by a patrician and hereditary patrimony above the wants of nature and the drudgery of office, sporting in the lap of pleasure, flattered, caressed and celebrated as a wit of the first order, he was easily prompted to exert himself, and to display those admirable talents which God had given him. His title, his fortune, a consciousness of his parts and popular character, seem to have been to him in the place of a good conscience; and he might be thought, by his manner, to have enjoyed all the peaceable fruits of righteoufnefs. A confidence in ourfelves naturally arifes from the approbation and applaufe of others; and few men living had more of that applaufe and approbation than Lord Chefterfield. In good humour with ourfelves, we are naturally impelled and properly qualified to fpread good humour among others: and it would be injuftice to his lordfhip to deny him the character of a pleafing and agreeable writer. As his fpirit was not cramped by a narrow fortune, fo neither was his temper foured by difappointment and diftrefs. Hence his wit is lively, gay, and frolic, and degenerates not into that fatyr, fpleen and invective, which generally mark the writings of difcarded and difcontented courtiers;

or,

SECTION I.

or, of those who think themselves neglected or injured, that is, denied somewhat, which their vanity suggests as due to their superior abilities and rank in life. He writes, therefore, not only with more freedom and security, but with ease, pleasure, and perfect epicurean tranquillity, to himself and to his friends; especially as the rule or principle which he prescribed to others, and which he practised himself, was to please.

Besides these advantages, he had his more manly faculties, his more valuable endowments, and his more solid virtues; so far as they were not melted down by that pleasure, that sweetness, those graces and that good humour, which we may presume, affected his style, as well as his con-

SECTION I.

duct: and we cannot help obferving that there is more eafe than elevation, more of fmoothnefs and foftnefs than of ftrength and vigour in his compofitions.

To the wit and genius which nature had lavifhed on Lord Chefterfield, he fuperadded application, critical knowledge and a ftudy of the beft writers on compofition and eloquence. Propriety and elegance of diction he had peculiarly cultivated, and moft earneftly recommends to his fon, as the drefs of thought, which had more power over the paffions and affections of mankind, than plain truth, reafon and argument.

A GENEROUS ambition had infpired him with an early tafte and love of letters,

letters, and with a contempt and neglect of field sports and the diversions of the turf, the fashionable amusements of his order. The first or best writers of Greece and Rome, poets, historians and orators, must be allowed, if not the foundation, yet the best models and masters of good sense, just taste and elegant composition; and to his classical enthusiasm among other causes, or to that academical pride and pedantry, which the courtier affects to despise and ridicule, we may justly ascribe that distinguished figure which Lord Chesterfield made, and still makes as a graceful writer and speaker.

To all this we may add, that he had supported some of the highest offices in the state, had conversed with courts and kings, and was familiar to

circles

circles of grandeur, magnificence and splendour. Hence we should not wonder that his style even upon ordinary occasions, and throughout the whole of this epistolary correspondence, is easy and unembarrassed, yet correct and elegant, enriched with apposite metaphors, and all the splendid and even gaudy ornaments of the polite scholar and accomplished courtier.

Thus nature and art, genius, birth and fortune conspired to form him a pleasing and persuasive orator; and a model of composition on prudential, on political, on familiar subjects. Upon the whole he is a masterly writer and judicious critic; on many subjects an entertaining, an instructive and very valuable author; especially where morality, the interests of sincere

cere virtue and the principles of true religion are not, immediately, concerned. But still he must be considered as a writer too easy, too smooth, too delicate and elegant to be numbered among the masters of eloquence; or to claim the title and applause of pathetic and sublime: he is more a wit than an orator, and has in his manner more of the shepherd's reed, or lover's lute, than the trumpet of the battle and the shouting. He wants the power to rouze, to awe, to animate and alarm, and resembles more the vernal breeze, or murmuring rill, than the tempest, the whirlwind, the lightening and thunder of heaven.

If it be said, that his literary correspondence did not afford a proper subject for eloquence and grandeur of com-

composition, we reply that the sublime does not so much arise from, or consist in the subject, as in the genius of him who has the molding of it; and that a soul devoted to delicacy, to politeness and pleasure is alike incapable of heroic deeds, of generous principles, of elevation of sentiment, and sublimity of diction.

We observe the majesty of Virgil frequently breaking forth in his eclogues, and we respect the prince of Roman poets, even in his shepherd's weeds. In his Georgics, it is observed by one * who was familiar with, and happily imitated his manner, " that we see in him a rustic majesty, like that of a Roman dictator

at

---

* Addison's Essay on the Georgics.

at the plough, that he delivers the meaneſt of his precepts with a kind of grandeur, and that he breaks the clods, and toſſes the dung about with an air of gracefulneſs." In other paſſages of his works, where he would ſeem moſt to depreſs himſelf, and to renounce all ambition, wealth and grandeur, he is, indeed, moſt admirable and elevated; as in the following paſſages.

Flumina
Amem, ſylvaſque inglorious!
Aude hoſpes contemnere opes, & te quoque dignum
Finge Deo.

From the great we naturally expect even in their triflings and amuſements, in their ſonnets and letters, an air of elevation and ſuperior dignity, ſuited to their birth, their titles and ſtation. Hamlet is ſtill the prince of Denmark

in

in his madnefs and extravagancies, even in his gallant *badinage* with Ophelia; and in his droll raillery with Polonius. Henry prince of Wales, amidft the blemifhes and irregularities which ftained the morning of his life, and connected, as he was with, that low and lewd buffoon Falftaff, ftill preferved and gave frequent proofs of confcious dignity and a princely fpirit, and fhone with a kind of clouded majefty that befpoke the brightnefs and glory of his future day.

As we have done fufficient juftice to Lord Chefterfield's ftyle and manner, (though we fay that he has more of Paterculus than of Livy, more of Xenophon than of Plato) fo we muft not pafs over his matter, without allowing its due claim to approbation and

and applause, on various subjects. He had from experience and reflection, a deep and extensive knowledge of human nature; particularly, of its follies, its weaknesses and vices; though of its great dignity, its rational powers, its intellectual attainments, its moral perfection and divine capacities he had no experience, and appears to have had no conception. But, on other subjects, that lie more within his sphere, he shews great knowledge, and makes not only pertinent and useful, but deep and refined observations.

In politics, so far as these were an art not connected with, nor founded in virtue, truth and conscience, Lord Chesterfield was a great proficient: for he had great masters; not indeed, a Livy

Livy nor a Clarendon, but the Cardinals Richlieu, Mazarine, De Retz, with Machiavel and Tacitus. These all made human nature, its follies, its frailties and falshood, the chief subject or inftrument of their operations; and admitted as lawful in the means, whatever was expedient to the ends they propofed.

On other fubjects, he is more moral, and therefore more inftructive and convincing. He has fhewn very good judgment in refpect to the bufinefs and conduct of the world; and fuppofing This to be our all, his lordfhip's advice in the acquifition and management of its profits and pleafures is perfectly œconomical and judicious. His prudential maxims, refpecting his pupil's future conduct in life, fpeak a difcernment

SECTION I.

ment perfectly acquainted with his subject, and an ardor and intenseness that had no other subject or object in view. No child of this world was, perhaps ever wiser in his generation than Lord Chesterfield; or prescribed more proper or effectual methods for making the most, or acquiring the largest share of it. Every child of the world, indeed, adopts the same conduct; but few, upon the comparison, have the same natural sagacity or acquired experience, to qualify them to prescribe the truest measures of such a conduct, or to cover the grossness and immorality of the practice, in some instances, with such plausibility of reasoning, such a semblance of prudence and such politeness of address.

The rules he gives respecting conversation

versation are perfectly just and rational: no one can more strongly paint, or more fully expose the folly, the impertinence, the ridiculous vanity of ordinary characters, in mixed company, than our well bred author. But these observations are such as the common sense of every one, who has been but moderately acquainted with the world, must dictate; and the noble lord, we may presume, from his clearness and justness in the preceptive, was himself a model in the practical part, and though vanity, by his own confession, had no little influence on his conduct, we may suppose that it did not make any part in his conversation. His observations on men and manners speak great sagacity; are just and clear, yet profound. They are only unhappily applied, when adduced

SECTION I.

ced as reasons to justify, to countenance or flatter the fashions, the follies and vices of mankind. Some of his remarks, however, are so trite and obvious to common observation, that they betray a simplicity of paternal fondness, and some seeming defect of understanding in a son who could want such admonitions. But we must remember that the father was, here, speaking to the son, and not to the public.

His observations on books and reading, on the use and abuse of time, on the end and advantage of travel,— on composition in general, and the epistolary in particular, are all perfectly just and truly valuable.

His advice to his son recommending

ing truth, virtue, honour and the purity of his moral character, we should have valued the more, had we not seen them afterwards explained away by court-casuistry, by the documents of politeness, by political logic, by an indulgence to pleasure and passion, to avarice and ambition, which the preceptor recommends elsewhere to his pupil: as the just contempt which the noble Lord pours upon the infidel tribe among us, had been of more weight, had he been less lavish of his compliments to some of the most eminent infidel writers.

If there is a fault in Lord Chesterfield's style, it is, that it is too much style. It has in it more of art than nature. Such an uniform construction of verbeage, the same rounded periods,

SECTION I.

periods, the same harmonious cadences, such a perpetual flow of wit and metaphor, with which his style is not only crouded, but, I had almost said, surfeited, like too luscious sweets, cloy rather than refresh us; and, we are disgusted with a vanity appearing in so much ornament and brilliancy of diction. Perpetual smoothness grows insipid: all softness, without a proper mixture of harsher, of stronger and bolder notes, affords but a languid pleasure; animates no noble passion of the soul, nor inspires any heroic or elevated sentiments.

THERE is a manly and spirited eloquence, equally removed from the cold correctness of the pedant, from the cant of a languishing *Inamorato*,

and

and the frippery of modish complaisance, as from the rudeness of the boor and the barbarism of a provincial dialect. This manly eloquence affects the heart more than the ear, the soul more than the sense, captivates nature with a happy violence and a power only less than divine.

THE simplest truth or object justly copied from nature, strikes you more than the most laboured or high coloured piece, in which you perceive the painter's intention was only to exhibit himself and to gratify his own vanity and ostentation. Lord Chesterfield generally preserves the tone of the great man, at least as much as could be expected in this familiar correspondence; yet, sometimes, he forgets himself, and falls below his proper

proper dignity: he is not only too lavish of, but has too much levity in, his wit: and in the perusal of these Letters we cannot always seclude the idea of the itinerant doctor, with that arch wag his buffoon, united in one person, acting, at the same time, the sage and the droll, and dispensing by turns his jokes and his pacquets.

WERE we to compare this famous collection of Letters with those of Tully or Pliny, we should say, That if our noble author is less entertaining and instructive, more barren and more abounding in repetitions than the two Romans; it may be observed in his defence, that he was more confined in his subject, and in his epistolary correspondence; nor does it appear that

that he wrote to the world, and with a view to its applaufe or approbation.

Cicero's and Pliny's Letters were wrote in form; frequently, on public occafions, and, to fome of the moſt eminent characters in Rome, diftinguifhed for letters and philofophy, for offices and honours. Lord Chefterfield's Letters are the inftant and unguarded effufions of his heart, rather than the ftudied compofitions of his head; and, though thrown off at random, give us a more real portrait of the noble Lord, than perhaps the moſt laborious and accurate pencil could have done. He is more natural and eafy, lefs fpruce, lefs laboured and affected than Pliny, but more oftentatious; and, as a wit, lefs ferious, lefs important, lefs moral, lefs less manly, less a Roman than Tully; whose Epistles are, we agree with Lord Chesterfield, perhaps the best models of composition, in this kind, of any yet extant.

Cicero, in his Epistles, gives us a variety of incidents and characters; and exhibits strong instances of his humanity and benevolence, by the advice, the support, the comfort he administers to some of his friends. and by the recommendation he wrote with, and the protection and favour he procured, for others. These friendly offices seem to occupy the greatest part of his literary correspondence. But in the Letters before us we are tired and disgusted with the same spirit of meanness and selfishness, which dictates every letter, I had almost

moſt ſaid every line of this corre-
' ſpondence, between the father and
his ſon, whom he inſtructs in the
practice of humanity and benevolence,
not as a duty, but an art or profeſſion
which he was to live and thrive by;
and who is taught to pleaſe and oblige
mankind, not for their own ſakes,
but to engage them to ſecond his own
views, and to promote his intereſt or
ambition.

NOTWITHSTANDING all the dignity which Lord Cheſterfield affects
and preſcribes, there is a conſpicu-
ous littleneſs in his general ſentiments
and directions, confined as they are,
in their ſubject, to the mere intereſt
of the two correſponding parties; as
if Lord Cheſterfield and his ſon were
the only two perſons worthy note;
or

or as if others were only confiderable in proportion to their capacity of ferving and obliging the father and the fon. Mankind muft be fomewhat mortified in confidering themfelves in the light, in which Lord Chefterfield has confidered them; as puppets and machines, which thefe two political jugglers are to manage and play off, as beft fuits their own interefts and occafions. He who exacts fo much attention to others, may feem to have no faculties, but for this his other felf: and we are hurt by an anxiety, as intenfely and ardently conceived and expreffed, for one beardlefs boy, as if the whole univerfe was concerned, or at ftake, on the advancement or mifcarriage of his future figure and fortune.

If

SECTION I.

If Cicero is accufed of having deferted his friends and the caufe of the republic, it fhould be remembered, that it was not before that caufe was defperate; and he has in his Letters frequently and warmly expreffed his zeal for the commonwealth, and lamented the wretched ftate of his country, " which had not one patriot left." But our noble author feems to confider corruption as an indifferent, or innocent thing: he talks of treating with the burrough jobbers, for the purchafe of a feat in the houfe, as a neceffary and ufeful expedient for the benefit of his fon; and appears to have confidered his country in no other light, than as that of a conquered province, on whofe fpoils its governors were to feed and fatten.

CICERO.

SECTION I. 43

CICERO has not, if I remember right, ufed one licentious or indecent thought or expreffion, except one; and this intended to expofe the lewd creature to whom it was applied, and who was the fcandal of Rome and of her fex; but abounds with leffons of truth, maxims of wifdom, and juft, moral, and political reflections: but the rankeft Epicurean could not well be more a Senfualift, more diffolute or more immoral than the Noble Lord in thefe epiftolary Lectures to his Son.

IF Seneca is a beau, as Lord Bolingbroke, I think, has ftyled him, he is of a different order to the Noble Lord under our confideration. The philofopher's foppery arifes from a greatnefs and fplendor of thought. If his unnatural rant is madnefs, it is virtue

run

run mad. If the philosopher is ambitious, his ambition appears in the many and excellent things which he has said in favour not of vice but virtue; in describing a perfection and sublimity of truth and morality, which mere human nature was never capable of; and in recommending stoical absurdity as a practical priciple. This was certainly a much more venial fault than what our Noble Author is guilty of, in the excessive care and cultivation of external grace and outward accomplishments, which he has prescribed, and in the relaxations which he has indulged to the appetites and passions of vitiated nature. For, surely, it is better to say fine things, that tend to purify and exalt, than such as are fitted to debase and corrupt. In the eye of truth and reason, of GOD and his
Angels,

SECTION I.

Angels, one Seneca is of much more value than a hundred Chesterfield's; and there is many a single letter in Seneca, that, in point of truth and virtue, out-weighs the whole mass of this prolix collection; whose real merit, in contributing to the sincere virtue and happiness of mankind, amounts not to the weight of a grain, or the value of a cypher.

But Roman or Heathen Moralists were not the authors suited to Lord Chesterfield's taste and passions. Though he had a great native stock of his own, yet he was more ambitious of borrowing from, and imitating the French, both in the delicacy of his manner, and in the refinement of his matter and sentiments. *La Bruyere, Rochefaucault, le Cardinal de Retz*, and *le Duc de de Sully*, were amongſt his principal maſters in morals and politics. He has particularly and very juſtly recommended *la Bruyere*, but is leſs exact in his ſentiments of truth and nature, leſs original in his manner, leſs moral in his reflexions, leſs various, entertaining, and inſtructive in his characters, leſs picturesque in his deſcriptions; and, if he has more wit and levity than the Frenchman, he falls ſhort of him in genuine humour and vivacity, in depth and penetration, and in his eſtimate of true virtue, perſonal merit, and real greatneſs.

THE Duke *de Rochefaucault*'s maxims are generally founded in the corruption of human nature, and deducible from that corruption. This is, in many inſtances, but not univerſally,

verfally, true; for, this would not only difcredit, but deftroy all the nobleft efforts, both of the divine and humane virtues. Yet the Lord Chefterfield has carried it ftill farther than this, and he would make vanity, felf-love, and the other immoral paffions, not only the real effects of the corruption of human nature, but the legitimate principles of human conduct. He profeffes, that he himfelf acted upon, and advifes his fon to act upon thofe principles. What may be confidered, in the Duke *de Rochefaucault,* as a mere *Jeux d'efprit,*—the effort and pride of genius, is embraced by our author as fober and philofophical truth:—or, if Rochefaucault is, perhaps, as licentious in his principles, he is more chafte and lefs offenfive in his expreffion, and offers
lefs

less outrage to decency and the common sense of mankind.

The Duke *de Rochefaucault* thinks justly and expresses himself happily on many occasions. Without the vanity of wit, or the ostentation of science and reading, he every where preserves the air of a sober inquirer and of the man of quality. He regarded himself as addressing the public: whilst Lord Chesterfield gave full range to his licentious spirit, secure, as he thought himself, from the notice and censure of the world.

Notwithstanding his great abilities and affectation to display his wit, Lord Chesterfield has many common place reflections, which had made a very indifferent figure in a writer of less
name

SECTION I. 49

name and note. You read many a page, I had almost said a volume together, particularly the last or fourth, with very little improvement or information; except of some private anecdotes and the news of the day, obvious to every observer as well as his Lordship, who confesses that he was not in the secret. As a man of taste, he disapproves trite sayings and vulgar observations; and warns his pupil to avoid them in conversation. They are as tedious, his lordship might have known, in books as in discourse. Yet, many of his maxims and moral documents are such as have been hackneyed and handed down, from father to son, for two thousand years past. His own frequent repetition of them tires us: but we grow sick of them, when we see them hashed over again,

E and

and served up anew, by a Reverend Doctor, whether for his own advantage, or for the benefit of the public, he knows best. The *Duc de Rochefaucault* has, indeed, the same sentiment running through all his books, but then it is expressed in such various language, and illustrated by so many various instances and examples, that we are rather entertained than disgusted with the noble author. His subject is, indeed, the most obvious and common, viz. the human conduct: but, the motives from which he derives that conduct, or, on which he founds it, have generally an air of novelty; and thus please, at least, if they do not inform and instruct the reader. *Rochefaucault's* maxims may be allowed, as many of them are, certainly true; yet be applied, contrary to, or beyond the

views

views and seeming intention of the author, to the support of true religion. For, while they expose the feebleness and imperfection, they mortify the pride of human virtue; they shew us the propriety of humility, with the necessity of the divine assistance to regulate our manners, and to form a just moral conduct; and whilst they strip us of a false splendor, that makes us vain, they teach us both the reality and greatness of a virtue, that is both humble and sincere. But Lord Chesterfield's sentiments and maxims, on moral subjects, are often directly subversive of the principles of both natural and revealed religion.

AN enthusiast would take *Rochefaucault* for a serious assertor, and an able defender of that extravagant puritanical paradox,

paradox, which ſtamps ſin, damnation, and death upon the whole moral and rational creation of GOD; whilſt Lord Cheſterfield might ſeem to regard thoſe maxims as founded in truth and the conſtitution of nature, and therefore a ſufficient excuſe for all the vice, folly, and immorality that abounds in the world; and poor human nature muſt, it ſeems, be an apology for all the weakneſſes and obliquities we are guilty of. Thus, though he who invades another's property is, according to his Lordſhip, juſtly hanged for it, yet he who invades or violates a property, which the owner may be ſuppoſed to hold moſt dear,—the virtue of his wife or daughter, may charge the fault on fortune or the ſtars. Such is the latitude in morality which the modern polite philoſopher permits and indulges.

SECTION I.

indulges. And, what could be the cause of this degenerate way of thinking in the two noble authors here compared, but a consciousness of their own frailties and vices, which they were willing to charge upon nature and necessity, and not to admit as their own act and deed?

But, perhaps, we have digressed too far in bringing into view the general character of Lord Chesterfield, when the professed design of this section was to exhibit the fairer side of it. But, so obnoxious is his moral character, that it is difficult to view him in any light without some degree of censure or prejudice.

SECT. II.

WE shall therefore be excused, if we indulge ourselves a moment longer in reviewing the amiable part of Lord Chesterfield's character, as it strikes us at first sight, and before we come to a nearer inspection and examination of his genuine form and features.

THE true character of the noble Lord is given us, by himself, in colours too striking to be mistaken. He was easy and pleasing in his diction, elegant in his manners, polite in his address, endowed by art and nature with knowledge to instruct, with elocution to perfuade, to charm, and captivate mankind. He had read books;— he had read men;— he was well acquainted with the workings of human nature, its various paffions and propenfities. Good breeding, and the art of pleafing, feem to have been the principal object of his ftudy; and thefe were made fubfervient to a darling ambition of fharing in the advantages, and fhining in the dignity and fplendor of high life, of popular admiration, and courtly magnificence. Educated in eafe and elegance, in polite letters and polite company, diftinguifhed by title and fortune, by wit and genius, we obferve his head impreffed with ideas, and his fentiments tinctured with a colouring derived from thefe various circumftances, and accidents of his life

SECTION II.

life and fortune. All is eafy and natural, except his wit, which appears, in the application, fometimes affected and extravagant, and indulged at the expence both of truth, decency, and virtue: the luxuriancy of his imagination made him prodigal of it. Animated, as he was, with the ambition of his fon's making a figure in courts, we naturally expect, and are not difappointed in our expectations, that a comprehenfive or a competent knowledge of the hiftory, the genius, the temper, the various conftitutions, laws, interefts and productions of the feveral ftates of Europe fhould be recommended to his attention and cultivation. His plan of ftudy on this fubject, though not regular or fyftematical, as communicated in fcattered hints with the eafe and familiarity of a friend, a friend, is yet rational and judicious, and is only too minute in the parts, and too extensive in the whole for the comprehension, or at least the perfect attainment of his young pupil; whose capacity he seems to have measured by his own, or by his partiality or his ambition for him: yet the noble author saw, that all this comprehensive knowledge would be of little use to the possessor, in public counsels or popular assemblies, without language to express, and the art and ornament of elocution to adorn and recommend his sentiments to his hearers. His reflections on taste in general, and on eloquence in particular, are accurate and instructive; and the effects ascribed to the last verified by pertinent and striking instances. Lord Chesterfield was himself, we may

fairly

SECTION II.

fairly presume, a great master in the art of speaking which he hear recommends.

Besides the foreign, the speculative and important knowledge proper and necessary for the forming of our young statesman, the noble author recommends, as still more necessary, the knowledge of human nature, and the learning and art practised in a court. The art of pleasing, of which he was a perfect master, he prescribes to his pupil as the most direct and useful ladder, by which he is to ascend to the honours and favours of a court, and to the distinction and eminence of a courtier. Other virtues may command respect and esteem; yet to please is the only way to command affection and love: — but to please, you

you must first know, you must first study mankind; a study in which the noble author seems to have been a great proficient, as might reasonably be expected from his constant application to it: yet, as was most suitable to his ambition, the highest orders of mankind were the peculiar and distinguished objects of his address and adulation. The manners, the honours, the splendor of courtly life had charms irresistible in his eye; here he moved most gracefully, as in his proper sphere; in an element in which he might seem to have been born and bred, and to have past all his days [*]. Here he presides as the genius of the place, and holds out a court-garment composed of all the

[*] Vol. III. p. 266.

insinuation,

SECTION II.

insinuation, the art, the address, the versatility, the respect, the condescension, the complacency, the sweetness, the ineffable graces, the elegancies and proprieties of polish and splendor necessary to be put on, and worn by all such who aspire to be favourites and ministers. As he affected to shine in all, and most in the best companies, it was here he found the best, that is, the most fashionable people, and most suited to his taste and ambition *.

His passions, his wit and imagination being unrestrained, unbroken and undisciplined, were naturally lead to full range, and to adopt objects the most pleasurable, the most pompous,

* See p. 274—282.

the

the greatest and most magnificent in life: thus we see not only his passions, but his very taste and judgment affected by the ply or bias which he had received from nature or education. Hence we account for the preference which he gives to French manners, both in life and on the stage, — to their delicacy, their softness, their versatility and complacency, before the rudeness and savageness of *British Bumkins*, or in other words, country squires, and before the bloody dramatic writers of his own country. He requires delicacy more than strength; pleasure rather than instruction; and the graces before all the other divinities in heaven or earth. Hence we account for the peculiar distinction of approbation and applause which he has given to the palace of *Alcina*

Aloina in *Ariosto*; and for his partiality to the eclat of *Voltaire*, and his History of *Lewis* the Fourteenth.

View then Lord Chesterfield in the the fairest, point of light, and you admire him as the fine gentleman, easy, elegant and polite, profuse of his complacency, blandishments, the most winning address and courteous condescension; expensive and fashionable in his dress;— splendid at his table, but not luxurious; voluptuous, yet not debauched; a libertine with decency; and in the midst of vagrant amours and illicit indulgences, still affecting the man of honour and truth;— refined, yet generally just in his taste, proper and elegant in his diction; powerful and persuasive in his elocution;

tion — largely converfant with, and a very good judge both of books and men; a great mafter in the extenfive fcience of politics, yet ftill more diftinguifhed as a courtier than a ftatefman; — fingularly eminent for his addrefs, his movements, his graces, the *douceurs*, the foftneffes, the placid features, the various airs, that habit of pleafing, that perfection of good breeding, which are natural to the foil, and form both the effence and exterior of a court.

OR in other words; thefe Letters, at the firft glance, exhibit Lord Chefterfield, and prefent him to the public as a kind mafter, an anxious and affectionate parent, an engaging companion, an obliging friend, a polite fcholar, a fine gentleman, a lively wit, an accomplished courtier, a penetrating statesman, a compleat man of the world, furnished with all the qualities, and adorned with all the graces that might promote his interest, or favour his ambition, that might render him easy in himself, and agreeable, respectable, or necessary to others; the man of sense, the man of virtue, and the man of honour; with genius, without singularity or affectation; with learning, without pedantry; with place and title, without pomp and pride; equally qualified for business, or for pleasure; for the cabinet, or the drawing-room; for a senate, or a private station; for a lady's levee, or a congress of princes. Such is the portrait of the noble Lord, as we may collect it thrown off in scattered touches and random strokes

SECTION II.

of his masterly pencil. Innumerable graces enter into the compofition of this effay towards perfection; and we have only to lament, that we find them, upon a nearer infpection, fo miferably fhaded and difgraced by the fouleft ftains, and the moft impure mixtures.

SECT. III.

IN the two laſt ſections, we gave, what we call, the bright ſide of Lord Cheſterfield's character: but we muſt not reſt here, if we would ſee his lordſhip's real portrait, and drawn at full length. Nor can the Peerage plead privilege at the bar of criticiſm. Not only truth, but the whole truth is exacted from us, when we would inform and inſtruct mankind. This is the more neceſſary on the preſent occaſion; as the character and example of Lord Cheſterfield, celebrated as he was for wit and virtue, might, otherwiſe, do miſchief, by propagating vice and vanity, folly and falſehood, among mankind. Besides, there is an ease, an elegance, and charm in his Lordship's style and manner, which may easily insinuate itself, and impose upon the common reader; as his plausibility imposed even upon the wise and good, in his life-time. Court-logic is, perhaps, as fallacious as the school-logic; and we are in much less danger of being misled in our conduct and manners, by the subtility of a rusty doctor, than by the refinement of a polite and well-bred man of distinction and family.

WHAT most offends us in these letters is, the immorality with which they are replete. As a moralist, indeed, he affects to recommend virtue and good faith; but he is quite out of his element on this subject, and seems to

SECTION III.

to have known no more of the effence, the power, the peaceful, and happy effects of virtue, than of what is doing in the moon, or any of the remoter planets: and the whole perfection he requires of his fon, is the very reverfe, not only of chriftian duty, but of true philofophy.

He confiders moral virtue and honour, as paffable qualities, and of fome name and reputation in the world; and as fuch he recommends them to his fon; but of the effential purity, the immutable nature, and eternal obligations of virtue, he had no conception; or if he had, he prefcribes practices, which he allows not ftrictly juftifiable; and avowedly indulges a violation of laws, both divine and human, in favour of your paffions, where you may escape the censure, by not contradicting the fashion and opinion of the world.

Virtue and religion have in them a sublime, a perfection, and divinity, which hold no friendly commerce with the common manners of the world. The man of the world is too much, and too eagerly engaged in the business and pleasures of life, to lend a proper attention to abstract and spiritual subjects; or to relish the investigation of moral, intellectual, and religious truth.

Lord Chesterfield's system of ethics is void of all sincere love to GOD or man, and may be properly styled a system of self-love. His Lordship is a remarkable proof of the truth of an observation, which he has more than once

SECTION III.

once repeated, That the underſtanding is the dupe of the paſſions. With an uncommon ſhare of underſtanding, enlarged and improved by reading and reflection, with all his wit, his ſtudies, and ſuperior ſagacity, he has ſacrificed the moſt uncontroverted principles and nobleſt efforts of virtue, love of your country, ſincerity to your friends, (which he ſcarce allows to have any exiſtence) a contempt of pleaſure, and vain glory, to a gratification of the ſelfiſh paſſions, to what ambition aſpires after, and to what the lower and animal appetites prompt. And the vices from which he would avert his pupil, are not repreſented in their native deformity, as violations of the laws of GOD, and of the ſanctions of men; as contrary to the opinions and practice of the beſt and
wiſeſt,

wifeft, and as deftructive of the principles of truth, and of the interefts of fociety; but, they are to be avoided from the confideration of their indelicacy, and the inconvenience and damage they bring to health, to fortune, and to your reputation in the world; fo far as your intereft may depend on that reputation, whether the world thinks right or wrong. Thus a common proftitute is forbidden, as what is dangerous and difgraceful; and keeping is condemned as what both the Indies could not fupport: but an intrigue with a *Whore of Quality*, married or unmarried, is a gallantry not forbidden; but propofed and inculcated by the father to his fon, as what, befides other advantages, is not difcreditable in the opinion of the world.

SOME

SECTION III.

SOME men's notions of virtue, and of the perfection of human nature, have been so sublime and refined, that their schemes being found impracticable, they have abandoned society and the world, to enjoy their ideal virtue in the shade. But Lord Chesterfield's notions of poor human nature are such, and his virtue of so easy and pliant a temper, that its very essence may seem to consist in its versatility, and conformity to the manners of those with whom you converse. Alcibiades's character, abandoned as it was, is, I think, proposed in this respect, as an example for his son's imitation; and a court, according to his Lordship, the grand scene of simulation and dissimulation, is the proper foil for the growth, the display and expansion of virtue.

SECTION III.

THE noble Lord's courtefy and humanity, overflowing and benevolent as they feem, are all a profufion of verbeage, or the art of faying the beft things, and offering your beft fervices, meaning and intending nothing, but to deceive thofe who are fimple enough to believe you fincere. For, to thofe who are in the fecret, and mutually practife this mechanical trade of compliment, without any meaning, it is the moft ludicrous farce in nature. Fie on it, my Lord! A fhame upon that policy, which makes no diftinction between prudence and artifice; between benevolence and flattery; between complacency and compliment; between wifdom and craft; between the modeft referve of the man, and the profeffed diffimulation of the courtier; which excludes fincerity and friend-

SECTION III.

friendship, true philosophy, true virtue and true religion ! *

VANITY, or an appetite for fame, which Lord Chesterfield has made the motive and foundation of morality, and acknowledges to have been the principal incentive to his good actions, is itself a vice; or a virtue, if a virtue, which must dispose the practiser of it to adopt every vice or folly in fashion. A steady perseverance in the practice of what is righteous, just and good,

---

* " UN homme qui fait la cour, est maitre de son geste, de ses yeux et de son visage, il est profond, impenetrable ; il dissimule les mauvais offices, soûrit à ses ennemis, contraint son humeur, déguise ses passions, dément son cœur, parle, agit contre ses sentimens : tout ce grand raffinement n'est qu'un vice, que l'on appelle fausseté."

M. DE LA BRUYERE, Tom. I. p. 224.

in opposition to the fashion and corruption of the world has, and we hope, will ever be considered in the estimation both of reason, and revelation, as one of the most signal instances, and highest exertions of true virtue: but Lord Chesterfield, we presume, was the first philosopher, who coolly and soberly recommended the fashion and corrupt opinions of the world, as the standard by which, and in conformity to which, you are to form your moral conduct. We cannot easily account for a nobleman of such admirable parts, advancing such outragious paradoxes; only this may be alledged in his favour, that he never published, nor surely ever intended that they should be published to the world: they are no more than his private sentiments,

SECTION III.

timents, contracted from his commerce with the world, and communicated in confidence to a particular friend, on whofe paffions they might eafily operate without oppofition from reafon or fcruple of confcience.

You have in Lord Chefterfield a perfect picture of a man of the world. He will make the moft of you, and of that world: he will affect your friendfhip; he will narrowly watch, and infidioufly pry into your infirmities; he will fifh out your fecrets, he will flatter your foibles; he will connive at, rather than reprove your faults: by a new invented diftinction between morals and manners he will recommend and reconcile every plaufible and enfnaring artifice in converfation and conduct,

SECTION III.

conduct, to the art of pleasing, to politeness, and political expediency*.

WE should not easily reconcile such a practice to the clear and sound understanding, and the candid and benevolent heart, which the Lord Chesterfield seems to be possessed of, had we

"*Soyez ambitienx, dit le monde á ses sectateurs, ufez de finesse envers vos egaux, de dissimulation envers le Grands, de rigeur envers vos inferieurs, ap renez á satisfaire vos passions d' une maniere dèlicate, instruifez-vous de la morale politique, fuivez ces guides qui vous conduiront au succès de vos galanteries, qui vous ouvrent les chemins de la faveur. Sacrifiez tout á votre agrandissement, point d' affectation dans votre probitè, si elle est contraire a votre reputation, point de probitè rèelle, si elle est nuisible aux desseins de votre fortune, suplantez cet ennemi, dètruisez ce rival, ne songez qu' á vous èlever. Telles sont les maximes de monde."

M. DE LA BRUYERE, Tom. 2. p. 36.

SECTION III.

not been told, and did we not obferve it proved to us by daily examples, that the love of the world blinds the eyes of men, obfcures their moral difcernment; and that avarice and ambition, licentioufnefs and lewdnefs generally difpofe thofe who are devoted to them, to evade or explain away the cleareft laws, and to refift the plaineft dictates of confcience, which contradict the indulgence of their favourite paffions.

SECT. IV.

AS Lord Chesterfield's monitions and observations are not arranged in any order, or distributed into regular Essays, but thrown off occasionally and at random, as the present thought or occasion suggested; so these Reflections are the sentiments which instantly and naturally presented themselves to the author, on an interrupted perusal of the noble Lord's epistolary correspondence. Nor is the reader to hope to meet in these remarks with the courtier, the flatterer, or the man of fashion; but the sentiments of a plain man, an Englishman, and a Christian, perhaps a little

little animated and warmed by the injuftice done, and the infult offered to morality, and the religion of his country, by the noble Lord. And as, we conceive, we have already done ample juftice to his abilities as a Writer, we think we have a right to take the more liberty, and to expect more credit and regard to our cenfures of him, as a Man and a Moralift.

MORALITY and Religion are too facred things to be fported away in wit; and the privileges, the comforts, the bleffings of human nature too valuable to be facrificed to the vanity or humour of the firft Peer or Prince in Chriftendom. The reverence in which I hold divine truth and the bleffed Author of my exiftence, will be my excufe, if I am not profufe profuse in my compliments to one, who however dignified and distinguished by rank and title, has shewn himself an offender against both. What strikes us at first sight, in these Letters, is the little efficacy which wit, reason, genius, erudition and education have in promoting sincere virtue, and establishing a just moral character, without the power and influence of religion. His Lordship has, indeed, frequently recommended integrity, and the moral virtues; but then he recommends them principally, if not solely, for the credit they give you with mankind, and as means fitted to serve your present interest, and to gratify your favourite passions; so that he occasionally indulges his pupil in the most immoral liberties, which are not disgraceful in the eye of of the fashion. The virtue he recommends is not such as you meet with in Plato, in Seneca, in Epictetus, or Antonine; such a virtue as may inform, improve, and fortify the soul, may support you under the calamities of life, push you on to heroic deeds, animate you in the cause of liberty and your country, or inflame your affections and beneficence to mankind; — but it is a selfish principle, a political *sagesse*, directed merely to serve your ends, and to second your views, in the attainment of what Lord Chesterfield had most at heart, as the best and only good — the emoluments of the present life.

OF eloquence he has said many fine things: and too much, perhaps, cannot be said in its favour, when it is employed in support of truth and virtue, in defence of the injured and oppressed, — to expose the pillager and betrayer of our country, and to assert and vindicate the common rights and liberties of mankind. But when this divine talent is recommended, as Lord Chesterfield has recommended it, as a proper instrument to captivate the popular applause, to render yourself necessary to government, and thereby to force yourself into employment, distinction and eminence; we despise the venal writer or speaker, who, with the faculties of an Angel, thus basely prostitutes himself to the highest bidder. Religion itself is recommended, as far as it is recommended, as giving you an additional security in the integrity of those who

are

SECTION IV.

are influenced by it, and with whom you have to deal.

He paffed for a patriot, yet the whole ambition of his foul feems to have been to form his favourite to the character and deftination of a courtier: It is not for Britain, for its laws or liberties;— but for *Mr. Stanhope's* graces, perfections, figure, and fortune, that our patrician is concerned. The whole plan of his education is directed and calculated to make a great, not a good man; a fhining, not an ufeful character,—or only ufeful to himfelf,— or to the public, only for the fake of that felf. To this end he recommends to him the femblance more than the fubftance of virtue; artificial mannners, polite addrefs, and all the fuperficial graces that might attract the regard and confidence of those he conversed with.

LORD Chesterfield is a wit, has grace and eloquence, and displays a large acquaintance with books as well as men; but with all this knowledge, he knew not GOD. He was too polite, had too much spirit to be a believer, and too much pride to clafs with the common herd of mankind *, in the adopting principles and

privi-

* " C'EST déja trop d'avoir avec le peuple une même religion & un même Dieu ; quel moyen encore de s'appeller Pierre, Iean, Jacques, comme le Marchand ou le laboureur : évitons d'avoir rien de commun avec la multitude, affectons au contraire toutes les distinctions qui nous en feparent ; qu'elle s'approprie les douze apotres, leurs disciples, les premiers martyrs (telles gens, tels patrons) qu'elle voye avec plaifir revenir toutes les années ce jour particulier que chacun celebre comme fa fête. Pour
nous

SECTION IV. 87

privileges which were common to him with his footman.

IF he warns his son against the common cant and raillery of infidelity against religion and established opinions, it is a caution, we presume, against ill manners, not expressive of any regard to sacred truth, or the principles of divine revelation: all his cautions

---

nous autres grands, ayons recours aux noms profanes, faisons — nous baptiser sous ceux d'Annibal, de Cefar, & de Pompée, c' étoient de grands hommes; sous celui de Lucrece, c' étoit une, illustre Romaine; sous ceux de Renaud, de Roger, d'Olivier & de Tancrede, c' étoient des Paladins, & le Roman n'a point de heros plus merveilleux; sous ceux d'Hector, d'Achille, d'Hercule, tous demideux; sous ceux même de Phœbus & de Diane: & qui nous empêchera de nous faire nommer Jupiter, ou Mercure, ou Venus, ou Adonis?"

M. DE LA BRUYERE, Tom. I. p. 264.

cautions of this kind, which recommend, or seem to recommend, virtue, are prudential, not pious. So pitiful a quality as piety must have for ever disgraced the character of the man of birth and breeding.

As a wit and a fine gentleman, he very properly proscribes vulgarisms, yet he has himself descended to one of the lowest ; — the unmanly railing at all womankind, from his commerce, we imagine, with the worst of the sex. It is certain that his Lordship's taste and reading had not led him to an acquaintance with the history of those ladies whose beauty was the least of their perfections ; — whose virgin sanctity or conjugal fidelity has done, and still does honour, to human nature ; — whose graces have contributed

SECTION IV.

ted to the order and ornament, the peace and happinefs of domeftic life; whofe councils have informed princes, whofe wifdom has directed the reins of empire, whofe prowefs has conducted armies, fought battles, and defended kingdoms;—whofe zeal and fincerity for the caufe of GOD, and his truth, have infpired them with the courage to brave danger and death, and to embrace the rack and the flames.

LORD CHESTERFIELD's calumny againft the whole female world is the more illiberal, unjuft, and inexcufable, as he beheld, with his own eyes, a living example of the foremoft of her fex, in rank and dignity, ftill more confpicuous and elevated by the purity,

the

SECTION IV.

the luftre, the majefty of her virtues. *

However, his Lordfhip might have been more confiftent in his cenfures. He had obferved in general, that " among women, as among men, " there are good as well as bad, and " it may be, full as many or more " good than among men;" and that " all general reflections, upon nations " and focieties, are the trite thread- " bare jokes of thofe who fet up for. " wit

---

* " You feem not to know the character of the " queen : here it is—fhe is a good woman, a good " wife, a tender mother ; and an unmeddling " queen." Vol. IV. p. 225.

The Critics feem to have been miftaken in apply-ing this character to the late Queen Caroline, who had been dead fome years, at the time of Lord Chef-terfield's writing this letter, which is dated July 2d, 1765.

SECTION IV.

" wit without having it, and fo have
" recourfe to common place." Nay
he elfewhere * prefcribes a particular
refpect to be paid to the ladies. Yet
after all this, polite and noble as he
was, he defcends to traduce the whole
fex, and expofe them in an odious
and contemptible light. But confiftency was no part of Lord Chefterfield's character as a writer, or he
would not have cenfured the late Earl
of Bath †, as long famous for his fimulation and diffimulation, and yet
have ferioufly recommended and juftified thefe qualities to his fon.

Thus too he cenfures thofe who
cenfure courts; yet he has himfelf
given fuch a picture of courts, as does
no honour to the learning, the truth,
and

* Vol. III. p. 205.
† Vol. IV. p. 211.

SECTION IV.

and sincerity of those who frequent them. If he is sometimes lavish of his praises in favour of the brilliancy. the politeness and perfection of court-life and court-breeding, he is not less frank in his report of the ill faith and ill morals practised there. It is only the appearance of good faith and good manners which he requires in those who would shine there: and the author, noble as he is, shews himself both illiberal and disingenuous, in the artifice he prescribes to be practised on the foibles and follies, the passions and prejudices of those you mean to engage in your service, and render conformable to your views.

His four volumes may be entitled, *An entire Code of Hypocrisy and Dissimulation;* containing the *finesse,* the artifice,

SECTION IV.

artifice, the craft, the virtue, or the semblance of virtue, with all the external accomplishments necessary to form the character of the complete Courtier. The christian, or, in other words, the sincere Moralist, will look upon the noble Lord, with all his wit, his genius, his elegance and penetration, as a little, a frivolous and superficial man; engrossed by selfishness, vanity and ambition; and in order to gratify these passions, a devout conformist to the world, its fashions and follies;— regardless of the interests or miseries of mortality, but so far as he may reap advantage from them, and profit by the follies or frailties of mankind.

THE virtue of the ancients was a sublime and splendid form, a beauty that

that captivated, and was made to captivate all hearts, — a divinity that challenged univerſal homage. The Roman virtue, in particular, was of a robuſt and maſculine form, affected exerciſe more than eaſe, and vigour more than delicacy. It confiſted in refiſting pleaſure and pain, in conquering paſſion, in embracing or honouring honeſt poverty, in deſpiſing riches and nominal honours; --- in an obſtinate adherence to truth and duty, in oppoſition to every terror or temptation. Roman virtue, the primitive, genuine, Roman virtue, the parent of liberty, of empire and glory, was undone by the graces and delicacies recommended by Lord Cheſterfield *; and degenerated to a fribble,

---

* HORACE, though licentious in his ſpirit, and epicurean in his practice, ſaw and acknowledged the bene-

ble, shuddering at every blast, and bending to every ruder assault from domestic tyranny and foreign invasion.

CATO would have exclaimed against the beneficial effects, and professed himself a friend, of true virtue; as he expressed his detestation of vice, in general, and of lewdness, in particular, as the source of that degeneracy which marked his own age, and which, in fact, was attended with the most baneful consequences to the republic.

> Fecunda culpae secula nuptias
> Primum inquinavere, et genus, et domos:
>   Hoc fonte derivata elades
>   In patriam populumque fluxit. ———
>
> ———————————
>
> Non his juventus orta parentibus
> Infecit aequor sanguine Punico,
>   Pyrrhumque, et ingentem cecidit
>   Antiochum, Hannibalemque dirum:
> Sed rusticorum mascula militum
> Proles, &c.
>   HORACE, Lib. III. Ode 6.

the manners and maxims of our British peer, as big with more certain and fatal ruin to the state, than a Cataline or a Cæsar. In Lord Chesterfield, the graces are to supply the place of the virtues. Real, sincere, substantial virtue, makes no part of his moral system; or where something like it is recommended, it loses all its worth and lustre by being directed to mere selfish and mercenary ends: and simulation and dissimulation, or a well-conducted hypocrisy, is prescribed as a succedaneum, equally or more effectual to captivate and ensnare mankind, than simple virtue, which a courtier might think too prudish and pedantic a quality to make any figure in the character and composition of a fine gentleman.—You may fight your man, or debauch your woman, if she

is

SECTION IV.

is but of quality; and nothing in all this amifs, while you conform to the fafhion and tafte of the world. Friendfhip is little more than a name, rarely to be found, and, therefore, not worth cultivating. The good opinion of the world is all that you have to confult: by fome means moft men are to be caught, all women almoft by any means. Therefore, you are to affect the confidence of every man, and the love of every woman you meet with, though you have no manner of refpect for the one, or for the other. Study above all things to be well with both, and make ufe of them as helps to ferve your intereft, and favour your ambition. Converfe with all, and watch their unguarded moments: domefticate with all, that you may hunt out the fecrets of families: affect the

friend-

friendship of all, that you may take the advantage of their confidence: apply all you know, and see, and hear, to your own profit. That you may penetrate the secrets, and acquaint yourself with the passions and views of a Prince, intrigue with his whore. Become all things to all men, that you may gain all.

VIRTUE, truth, and good sense, according to Lord Chesterfield, are not so much to be studied as eloquence; for by this last you will most advantage yourself: and if you are enjoined to lay in the largest stock of knowledge, it is not the better to enable you to serve your King and Country, but that these may serve you. Some of these political maxims might be proper instructions to a professed spy, but are

far

far below, and inconsistent with the dignity of one, who is sent abroad under a public character, to represent the honour, and vindicate the rights of a nation.

It has been said, by some who have perused these letters, that Lord Chesterfield hath left it in doubt with the world, whether he had any religion or not. I think there is no doubt remaining on this head. He has not, indeed, like Lord Bolingbroke, attacked the principles of religion in form, nor explicitly declared himself an unbeliever; yet it is plain, from the whole tenor of these letters, and the advice given to his dear friend and son, that he would have him consider this world as his all, and the prosecution and attainment of its pleasures and profits, its honours and dignities, as the one thing needful. Would a father, who knew his fon born for life and immortality, have been fo anxious for two inches added to his ftature? Would a father, who knew his fon intended for the purity and perfection of Angels, have prefcribed to him a conformity to this world, and an attachment to its pleafures and interefts, as the proper qualification and preparation for the next? Would a father, who had confidered his fon as an heir of glory, have confined all his attentions, affiduities, and attainments to that frail bubble, the glory of this world? Could a father, who was perfuaded, that an immortal fpirit informed his fon, betray fo much anxiety for the figure and ornaments of the body; for the dreffing of the hair,

and

SECTION IV.

and the pairing of the nails, of his immortal boy? Could the Noble Lord, with proper notions of the infinite and all-perfect GOD, as the best and supreme good, have fixed all his attention and affections on the favour and friendship of the world? Could any man, I say not of a religious spirit, but of a truly philosophic taste, centre all his hopes, his affections, his concern, his very heart and soul, on an indulgence to vanity, to pleasure, to interest, and ambition? These Letters exhibit not the moral man, but the man of the world; not the patriot, but the courtier: and the ruling passion of the Noble Lord seems to be, that of an aspiring statesman, or an ambitious conqueror, to figure it in the eyes of mankind. Only, here, the passion is conducted with more policy and prudence, than commonly falls to the lot of conquerors and favourites; who, generally, with lefs art and more violence, ufurp upon the common rights of mankind.

The Noble Lord, in the advice he has given, and the profpects and temptations he has laid before his fon, has fhewn himfelf as much a religionift, as the devil did, when he offered to the Saviour of mankind the kingdoms of this world and their glory.

One important leffon, which we may, however, learn from the letters before us, is this: That noble birth, great natural abilities, a polite education, and much reading and reflection, uninfluenced by religious motives, and
directed

SECTION IV.

directed to no religious end, render the poffeffor a poor and contemptible creature, a faithlefs friend, a falfe patriot, an immoral philofopher; and, in refpect to the trueft virtue, the fublimeft knowledge, and the moft important privileges of our nature, leave him poor and miferable, and blind and naked; and, in point of real dignity, rank him lower than the loweft of the fervants of the Carpenter's Son.

SECT. V.

LORD Chesterfield is allowed to be a wit; but his wit is unchastised, and licentious; is sometimes indulged out of mere vanity, in violation of truth; and, we presume, against his own better knowledge: it is, however, sometimes delicate, though frequently blunt and rude; and such as might better become a licentious companion over his bottle, than the polite scholar writing, at his ease, a course of moral lectures, for the benefit, instruction, and improvement of his son.

With very lively parts, and amidst pleasu-

pleasurable amusements, his application and study seem to have been very considerable. He read much, but did not think intensely. He was more pleased with what struck his imagination, than studious of what might regulate his passions, amend his heart, or inform his understanding. His literary acquirements were indeed uncommon for a man of quality. He seems to have well understood the state of modern, of polite literature, both at home and abroad; and from the large fund of materials, which he had laid up in his various and extensive reading, he criticises justly, he quotes pertinently, he applies happily. His observations on the English and French drama are perfectly just and judicious; though we think he has not done sufficient justice to the sublime

SECTION V.

lime spirit which distinguishes some of our own dramatic writers. In this case he has acted against his own prescript on another occasion, and has been more studious to find faults than point out beauties. His taste was somewhat vitiated, as his manners were corrupted, by his attachment to the French. We deny not, nor dispute the justice of the applause he has given to *Boileau*, *Moliere*, *Corneille*, and *Racine*. But the encomium he has given to *Voltaire*'s history of the age of *Lewis* the Fourteenth, we think altogether partial, and unworthy the good sense, and moral discernment of the Noble Author. To justify this censure, and to prevent the ill effects which Lord Chesterfield's admiration of this sprightly writer may have upon the English reader, it may not be amiss,

or

or improper, to strike off, *en passant,* a short critique upon this celebrated work; as it appears to a plain man, and a sober Englishman, to one who is better acquainted with ancient than modern manners, and more enamoured of the virtues than the graces. Lord Chesterfield's letter to Mr. *Voltaire,* so far as it relates to the history, or age, of *Lewis* the Fourteenth, is as follows:—" Permit me, Sir, to
" return you thanks for the pleasure
" and instruction I have received from
" your history of *Lewis* the XIV. I
" have as yet read it but four times,
" because I wish to forget it a little
" before I read it a fifth: but I find
" that impossible: I shall, therefore,
" only wait till you give us the aug-
" mentation which you promised:
" let me entreat you not to defer it
" long.

" long. I thought myself pretty con-
" versant in the history of the reign
" of *Lewis* the XIV. by means of
" those innumerable histories, me-
" moirs, anecdotes, &c. which I had
" read relative to that period of time.
" You have convinced me that I was
" mistaken, and had upon that sub-
" ject very confused ideas in many
" respects, and very false ones in
" others. Above all, I cannot but
" acknowledge the obligation we have
" to you, Sir, for the light which
" you have thrown upon the follies
" and outrages of the different sects;
" the weapons you employ against
" those madmen, or those impostors,
" are the only suitable ones; to make
" use of any others would be imitating
" them: they must be attacked by
" ridicule, and punished with con-
                            " tempt.

" tempt.—Give me leave, Sir, to tell
" you freely, that I am embarrassed
" upon your account, as I cannot de-
" termine what it is that I wish from
" you. When I read your last histo-
" ry, I am desirous you should always
" write history.—Adieu, Sir, I find
" that I must admire you every day
" more and more; but I also know,
" that nothing ever can add to the
" esteem and attachment with which,
" I am, &c*." This cannot be called a mere compliment, paid by a
friend to an author, upon a new pub-
lication, as Lord Chesterfield has repeated his approbation and applause of
Mr. *de Voltaire*'s works in general, and
of this in particular, in other letters
to his son.—How just this encomium

* Lord Chesterfield's Letters, Vol. III. p. 346-7.

is,

SECTION V.

is, may appear by the few following strictures.

Honesty, or a severe regard to truth, should be an essential ingredient in the composition of an historian. There are several remarks, in this history, on the Pope, the Cardinals, and Jesuits, which would incline one to think the author was sincere and open: but when we consider the privileges claimed by the Gallican Church, and find the Pope humbled by *Lewis* the Fourteenth, we suspect our author is but paying a compliment to his country, and would *seem* rather an enemy to the court, than to the Church of Rome: I said *seem*; for, at the bottom, I believe him a friend to no denomination of christians, though he has bolted out heretic and
schismatic

schifmatic upon occasion, and branded with infamy men better than himself.

I NEED give you no other proof of his dishonest conduct, than by referring you to his chapter of Calvinism; and will only quote you his own words, without troubling you with other authority, to confront the assertions, and set aside the falsehoods of this writer.

IN the beginning of this chapter he calls Calvinism (some might infer Christianity) a new pest, which has laid waste the world: he derives it from the republican spirit, which animated the first churches. This, though we do not call it a plain falshood, we know is not agreeable to truth: for, never were better subjects than the primitive christians. But his design is

SECTION V.

is to stigmatize all the Protestant Churches. And for what reason? Because they formed the strongest bulwark against the encroachments of his immortal hero, and were resolved to live independent of a temporal and spiritual tyranny.

BUT let us consider the crimes of these persecuted people; and thence we may best judge of the equity of their punishment. *Lewis*, says our historian, was exasperated at them. What was the cause, will our historian say? Were they in rebellion against their Prince? Did they call in foreigners to invade the kingdom? Or did they refuse the payment of taxes laid upon them? He says, no such thing. But the King was moved by the continual remonstrances of his clergy; by the insinuations of the

Jesuits and the court of Rome, by the Chancellor *Le Tellier*, and by *Louvois*, his son. " *Lewis*," it is to be confessed, " was wholly a stranger to the " fundamentals of their doctrine, and " regarded them as *old revolters.*" *Voltaire* himself allows, that during the factions of the *Fronde*, and the civil wars excited by the Princes of the Blood, the Parliament and the Bishops, they observed a pacific conduct, and made offer of their service to the King. He further owns, that *Colbert*, the Great *Colbert*, protected them as useful subjects; and that *Mazarine* was so sensible of their good conduct, that he admitted them into all the offices depending upon the revenue: nay he says, that though their fathers had been rebels under *Lewis* the Thirteenth, their sons were become good subjects under *Lewis* the Four-

SECTION V.

Fourteenth. Those very madmen (so he calls the reformed of the *Cevennes*) would never have taken up arms without the revocation of the Edict of *Nantze*. That they had not been in any eminent manner obnoxious to the government, appears from this, That their churches, according to Mr. *Voltaire*, were taken from them on the most slender pretexts, upon the most *frivolous pretences*[*]; and that the oppressions they laboured under, were covered over with a *form of justice*; — the highest aggravations, I should think, to an honest man's misery.

But his best reason for this persecution of the Protestants is still behind. *Lewis*, it seems, considered it as one of those enterprizes, which

---
[*] P. 206—209.

was productive of that lustre of glory, of which he was in all things fond even to idolatry *. And thus confiscating their estates, depriving them of their children, imprisoning, dragooning, hanging, and breaking upon the wheel, or burying alive, are lawful and justifiable, as being the merciful means employed to aggrandize the monarch's glory, and to make converts to the charitable religion of Jesus Christ.

Some tender expressions of humanity should, one would think, upon this occasion, have dropt from a writer, who seems charmed with delicacy of taste, softness of manners,

* P. 213.

SECTION V.

the cultivation of the graces, and the endearing charms of social life.

A BIGOTTED Heathen, familiar to the sight of Christians exposed in the Theatre to the hungry jaws of wild beasts, could not have expressed less pity for the sufferers, than our enlightened Philosopher, our abhorrer of Christian blood, does at the recital of such merciless inhumanity.

YET, all this while, the sufferers are in the fault. It is the pretended reformed religion, and its dogmatic spirit, that occasions this bloodshed: the orderers and executors of such hellish tragedies are free from blame. " Such," says he, " was the nature " of Calvinism, that it necessarily pro-
" duced civil wars, and shook the
" founda-

"foundation of ftates." Whereas the remark fhould have been, had he drawn his conclufion from his premifes; 'Such is the nature of Popery 'and falfe glory, that they deftroy 'humanity, cancel even the obligation 'of natural religion, facrifice thou-'fands without remorfe or pity, and 'deluge kingdoms with chriftian 'blood.'

And fuch, I will add, is the nature of infidelity, that it fwallows the grofleft falfhoods, and publifhes them to the world, and mifreprefents and prevaricates without fear or fhame. An Infidel is fitted for any caufe, but that of truth; will even defend Popery, though he denies Chriftianity, and adore a tyrant, though he defpifes GOD.

SECTION V.

When firſt I took up *Voltaire*, and had read ſome pages, I conſidered him as a ſprightly writer, with a tender heart, and thought him a lover of mankind: but his chapter of Calviniſm ſoon convinced me what was his humanity; as the court and character of *Lewis* ſhew what was his morality. He writes like a man of mode, and has formed his politics and his morals, not from books, but from his commerce with the world.

Policy of any ſort, righteous or unrighteous, if it be but ſuccefsful, is with *Voltaire* and with *Lewis* wiſdom; and corruption is an honeſt art: eclat is glory, though it be but the parade of guilt: and conqueſt is greatneſs and happineſs, though it is founded on injuſtice, and might render millions miserable. The reign of *Lewis,* when considered in a true light, and divested of the false colours which the historian has bedaubed it with, was the reign of pomp and pleasure, of corruption and ambition, of madness and misery. His glory was false, because his virtue was not true. Vanity was his supreme passion, and to be talked of, his supreme delight. Justice and humanity were trifles in the way of his ambition. Whatever was profitable and conducive to the ends he proposed, was to him lawful: goodness was a silly name, not heard of at court, and supplanted by that phantom glory. Virtue was not cultivated, but splendor was studied. The depth of others' misery was the height of *Lewis*'s glory. Greatness was in *Lewis*'s eye, and in his historian's, rian's, the shewy pomp of arms and conquests, not the harvest reaped from great and good actions done, or miseries suffered in the cause of virtue, for the support of truth, and for the sake of public happiness, tranquillity and safety.

WHAT is shining, affects *Voltaire* more than what is solid; or he is all the while talking or writing against his better knowledge; gilding ambition, lust and folly with polite appellations, and sacrificing religion, virtue and truth to the idol of *Lewis*'s glory. His flattery of the monarch is really too gross and apparent, and very ill becomes a writer of so free and ingenuous a spirit. He seems to be playing the sycophant to the living,

rather

rather than writing an impartial history of the dead.

His partiality to his country is as evident, as the Duke of Marlborough's victories are poorly and malignantly told: while *Turenne*'s fine campaign is sure to be celebrated: and yet this was more signalized by the fire, devastation and misery he spread, than by one battle fought or gained by superior courage and conduct. And I believe any one, truly acquainted with the particulars of this ravage, and the cruelties exercised in the Palatinate, will call *Turenne* a dog of hell, rather than a Christian hero. Yet this, it seems, was but a spark, compared to the second desolation of it. *

* P. 254.

As

SECTION V. 223

As a writer, I confess that Mr. *Voltaire* is lively and entertaining. He has not the phlegm of the English. He is sometimes happy in surprising his reader, and is fortunate in contrast and comparison. He is an admirer of wit, of which he has been all his life a careful collector: he has taken pains in secret history, and would, I dare say, take more pleasure in finding a modern anecdote, than in recovering a fragment of Plato or Livy. He would have made a rhetorical preacher, an ostentatious actor; and a better favourite at court, than a statesman, as he loved intrigue more than business: as a gentleman, he would have been enterprizing; as a minister, a lover of wit, pleasure, and pomp, a promoter of arts, and an encourager of science. In love, he would have been
gallant

gallant and romantic; in an embaſſy, generous and ſplendid.

He is better verſed in modern manners and modern politics, than in the true knowledge of human nature, or the ſpirit of ancient legiſlation and ancient heroiſm. True virtue, and the diſtinctions of moral good and evil, are ſcarce perceivable in his book. Feaſts, carouſals, magnificent pleaſures, the ſplendor of diverſions, delightful entertainments, polite arts, polite converſation, refinement of taſte, vivacity and wit, a decent gallantry, noble gallantry, eaſe and elegance, are in our Chriſtian Hiſtorian of the ſame eſteem and credit, as contempt of pleaſure, contempt of riches, inviolable chaſtity, honeſt poverty, ſevere juſtice, extenſive goodneſs, courage

SECTION V.

rage unappalled, a love for our country, and reverence for the gods are in our Pagan Livy. And hence it is,—Though he has not directly attacked virtue, yet he has bestowed abundant colouring and ornament on vice. Guilt is no more than gallantry; and greatness of soul (who could believe it?) is to change a mistress with discretion, and without distracting public business.*

THE fashion seems to have been with *Voltaire* the standard of morals; and the graces of more value with him than the virtues. Have but delicacy and politeness, and our author will not question your faith or your religion. One reason of his antipathy

* Vol. II. p. 47.

to Calvinism is, that it is pedantic, and betrays a savageness of manners. His religion is as bad as his morals, a vague detail of rash doubts, formed from common appearances: he seems to have known as little of true philosophy, as of true virtue, and to have borrowed his religion, as he has done his ethics, from the gentle systems of modern free-thinking; which are, indeed, well suited to a witty Frenchman, who is too lively to reason, and too gay to think.

It is difficult, he tells us, to determine what it is that gains or loses battles *. At other times he says, that our conduct and our enterprizes depend absolutely on our natural dis-

* Vol. I. p. 86.

SECTION V.

positions, and our success upon fortune*. He gives us more instances than one of the power of chance in deciding battles. At other times he is divided between fate and fortune; but this last seems to be his favourite; terms, which he substitutes in the room of Providence. "Fortune," says he, "did that (the restoration of "Charles the Second, of England) "which these two ministers, *Don* "*Lewis* and *Mazarine*, might have "had the glory of undertaking, &c." But hear what our noble Lord Clarendon says upon this occasion, a writer who saw far into the ways of GOD and man; and who, in respect of genius and knowledge, as well as virtue, is as much to be preferred to

* Vol. I. p. 42.

Voltaire,

Voltaire, as Socrates is to Lucian. " The King's condition was, he fays, " concluded to be in a ftate of defpair, " till men were confounded by fuch " an act of Providence, as GOD hath " fcarce vouchfafed to any nation, " fince he led his own chofen people " through the Red Sea*." And afterwards; " In this wonderful manner, " and with this incredible expedition, " did GOD put an end to the rebel- " lion that had raged near twenty " years :" and again, foon after; " By " thefe remarkable fteps among others, " did the wonderful hand of GOD, " in this fhort fpace of time, not only " bind up, and heal all thefe wounds, " &c. †" He had before told the

---

* Clar. Vol. VI. p. 691.
† Vol. II. p. 772-3.

SECTION V.

reader, " that the whole machine [of
" the reſtoration] was ſo infinitely
" above his [the General's] ſtrength,
" that it could be only moved by a
" Divine hand; and it was glory
" enough to his memory, that he was
" GOD's inſtrument in bringing thoſe
" mighty things to paſs; which, doubt-
" leſs, not one man living had of him-
" ſelf, either wiſdom to foreſee, or
" underſtanding to contrive, or cou-
" rage to attempt and execute *."

Now, which of theſe two hiſtorians
deſerves moſt credit upon this ſubject?
He who was a living witneſs, and a
careful obſerver of the tranſactions
of thoſe times; who was preſent
and privy to every meaſure taken to

* P. 708.

promote

promote or retard the restoration, and who had a large share of learning, both human and divine?—Or he who writes near a hundred years after the transaction, talks by hearsay, and judges at random, who retails the dregs of Epicurus for the object of our faith, and gives us the froth of modern free-thinking for the history of philosophy?

In the thirty-third chapter, he condemned some doctrines of Jansenius, as neither philosophical nor consolatory. And will he call his system of a world, governed by chance, philosophical? Or will mankind think his principles, by which they are left to nature, fortune, or fatality, consolatory? It has, I confess, surprized me much, and gives us a melancholy prospect

SECTION V.

prospect of the state of our morals and religion, to hear that the demand for this book has been so great. What has not that nation to fear and expect, which can laugh under the gloom of scepticism, and delight in misery and no GOD!

IT will be said, his character as a wit, and an entertaining writer, has recommended him.

I OWN he has some merit as a writer, but it is greatly overbalanced by his licentiousness as a moralist. Nor can I allow his talent at writing so eminent, as by the success of his book it might be judged. He has as much vanity, but more levity, than Tacitus: but, at the same time, he has more good nature, could we strike out his chapter of Calvinism. His very good nature, seems rather a national, or a constitutional gaiety, never checked by misfortune, nor qualified by distress, but enlivened by converse, wit, and the Belles Letters, than a rational humanity, founded on the principles of reason and religion.

His remarks are sometimes just, but they are sometimes notoriously false: generally please, rather than edify; and, are fitted for surprize, rather than instruction. He is smart, rather than solid; lively, than witty; airy, than sublime; and more florid than deep: a sceptic in his principles; a sophist in his arguments. In words, an assertor of morality; in fact, a destroyer of it. A professed admirer of philosophy, which he recommends from

modern

SECTION V.

modern discoveries, while he is really an asserter of ancient epicurism. He is an enemy to religion, and theology, from the accidental mistakes which the professors of both have been guilty of. The unhappy effects flowing from the perverseness of nominal christians; the mischiefs committed by faction and ambition, wearing the masks of religion, he lays to the charge of religion and christianity in general.

In short, you meet in *Voltaire*, with a false virtue, a false wisdom, a false happiness, a false heroism, and a false glory; and at the bottom of all, not the best heart.—I mean a heart not imbued with true religion, the only foundation of whatever is wise, and great, and good, and happy, in human nature.

SECT. VI.

FROM Mr. *dé Voltaire*, let us return to Lord Chesterfield. His regard for his friend, --- the brilliancy of the court of *Lewis* the Fourteenth, with the pomp and magnificence of the great monarch --- propitious as he was to science, to taste and genius, and the noble Lord's distinctions between moral good and evil, being depraved by his commerce with the world, might possibly influence him in his judgement, in the applause he has given, and the admiration he has expressed for this work of *Voltaire*.

How far this commerce with the world

world can influence the judgment, is abundantly clear, from the faithful portrait, which the noble Lord hath given us of himſelf, and from the honeſt confeſſion he has made, in the courſe of theſe Letters, of his own practice and principles;—a confeſſion which we ſhould have valued, and a portrait which we ſhould have admired the more, had he not affected to juſtify both the principles and practice by a ſhew of reaſon and argumentation.

THE dreſſing of the hair, the ſtrapping of the ſhoes, the cleaning of the teeth, and the pairing of the nails, may be matters of moment, and, in his Lordſhip's phraſe, " of infinite importance," worthy the care and attention of a fribble, but ſeem below the

SECTION VI.

the singular notice of a moralist and a philosopher: but, to recommend interest, self-love, vanity and ambition, as the proper motives of action, is, we conceive, an insult upon common sense, and upon all the moral systems that have yet been published to the world; except we might perhaps justify it by the tenets of Epicurus: and if we should despise the philosopher, we must both despise and abhor the patriot, who should defend or advance such principles as have their foundation in the corruption of our nature, and terminate in the destruction of public virtue, public liberty, and public happiness. His roundly pronouncing* Curtius and Leonidas to be two distinguished madmen, is such

* Vol. I. p. 321.

an outragious contradiction to established notions, to our clearest ideas of the purest and sublimest virtue, and such a blasphemy committed against the spirit of patriotism, as will never be forgiven him by any classical or moral reader, by any lover of GOD, or of his country. "Greater love, than " this, hath no man, that a man lay " down his life for his friends," is one of those maxims of eternal truth, not peculiar to, though most signally illustrated by, the process of the Christian dispensation, and by the life and death of its divine Author, but which approves itself not only to the most perfect reason of individuals, but to the common sense and natural feelings of evey age and nation upon earth; who have considered, and sometimes revered, as something more than mortal,

tal, thofe heroes and patriots, who have devoted their lives to the falvation of their country. Courtiers, as well as patriots, with the flattering friends, and the factious enemies of the ftate, have generally been afhamed of, and difavowed all felfifh principles, and affigned the public good as the motive of their conduct and councils; and nothing, we prefume, but the profpect of fecrefy in thefe confidential Letters from a father to a fon, could have induced the noble Lord to advance and avow fuch principles.

But there is nothing we can wonder at, in the principles of Lord Chefterfield, after we have feen the patrician and the father defcend from his dignity and duty, and commence procurer and pander to his fon;—
acting

acting the part of a bawd, and giving him direct lessons of lewdness: he marks down, he springs the game for him; he cheers him in the chace, by assuring him of success. From a nobleman so distinguished for delicacy of sentiment and manners, we could not have expected that an illicit and promiscuous commerce of the sexes would have been recommended or connived at, or that passion and brutal lust would have been allowed, as the motive and measure of human conduct, in violation of the order and peace of society, and in contradiction to the dictates of uncorrupted * nature and reason.

WHEN

---

* DEINDE quum M. Claudius circumstantibus matronis iret ad prehendendam virginem, lamentabilisque eum mulierum comploratio excepisset, Virginius,

SECTION VI.

When he proposes self-love, vanity, interest and ambition, as the proper motives to human conduct, he affects to make some apology, and to offer some reasons in vindication of his paradoxes : but in the libertine advice he has given to his son, he uses no ceremony, nor palliates his advice, as if conscious of its impropriety or immorality. We should naturally hence conjecture, that the noble, Lord had neither wife, sister, or daughter, in whose virtue he might think his own happiness and honour, or the honour

---

ginius, intentans in Appium manus, " Icilio," inquit, " Appi, non tibi filiam despondi : & AD " NUPTIAS, NON AD STUPRUM EDUCAVI. PLA- " CET PECUDUM FERARUMQUE RITU PROMIS- " CUE IN CONNUBITUS RUERE ? Passurine hæc " isti sint, nescio, non spero esse passuros illos, " qui arma habent."
   Liv. Lib. III. p. 182. Edit. Hearne.

and

and happiness of his family any way concerned.

In comedy and romance we have sometimes loose scenes exhibited, loose sentiments expressed, and lewd characters and examples held out to us, as copies or pictures of ordinary life, and the real manners of the times :--- but lessons of lewdness given professedly and coolly by a father to his son,--- pleasure taught and recommended as a necessary expedient in business, is such a novelty and refinement in the system of good breeding, is such an outrage done to decency, and to the moral sense generally entertained by mankind, so contrary to nature, and the usual workings of parental affection, that we cannot easily account for it, unless we might

be

SECTION VI.

be allowed to suppose, that the father, by engaging the son in the same criminal commerce, intended to flatter or justify their common conduct, and to detract from the infamy of both.

But, perhaps, there is some injustice in this last reflection. Lord Chesterfield appears not conscious of any infamy from his illicit commerce with the other sex, or that any dishonour attended the illegitimacy of his son; whom he published, not without some pride, in most of the courts of Europe. The truth may seem to be this. He writes, to use his own expression, as a man of pleasure to a man of pleasure: but being, as he acknowledges, past the quick sense of it himself, he was perhaps willing to refresh his imagination by dwelling

SECTION VI.

on the gallantries of his fon, and by renewing the memory of his own amours. * Nothing is more common than

THE fentiments of the excellent *Saurin* will both explain and confirm our reflections on this occafion : On ne s' abandonne pas ainfi á fes fens fans y avoir de la douceur : & ce qu' il y a de plus funefte, c'eft que cette douceur que l'on goûte, demeure dans le fouvenir, fait des traces profondes dans le cerveau, frappe l'imagination. ——— Si l'action des fens n' étoit exciteé que par la préfence des objets : fi l' ame n' étoit agitée que par l'action des fens, un feul moyen fuffiroit pour fe garantir des paffions : ce feroit de fuïr l'objet qui les émeut. Mais les paffions font d'autres defordres encore. C'eft cette forte impreffion qu' elles laiffent dans l' imagination. Lors qu' on f'eft abandonnè á fes fens, on a goûtè de la douceur : cette douceur frappe l'imagination ; & l'imagination ainfi frappèe des plaifirs que l'on a trouves, en rapelle le fouvenir, & follicite l'homme paffionnè de retourner vers ces objets qui lui ont été fi doux.

C'EST pour cela que les vieillards ont encore quel-

SECTION VI.

than this procefs in the depravity of human nature. We have feen, in other inftances, befides this before us, the

quelquefois des reftes malhereux d'une paffion qui femble fuppofer certain conftitution, & que l'on croiroit éteinte, dés que cette conftitution n'eft plus. Cette pénfée, que tels & tels objets furent la caufe de leurs delices, eft encore chere á leur ame : ils en aiment le fouvenir ; ils les font entrer dans tous les difcours ; ils en font des portraits flatés, & fe dédommagent en racontant leurs plaifirs paffés, de ce qu' ils leur font interdits par la vieilleffe. C'eft pour cela encore qu'il eft fi difficile á un homme qui a donné tête baiffeé dans le monde, d'y renoncer au lit de la mort. Il eft vrai qu'un corps accablé de maux, une nature prefque éteinte, des fens entierment amortis, femblent peu propres a laiffer dans un homme de l'amour pour les plaifirs fenfibles. Mais cette imagination frappée par les impreffions des plaifirs paffés, lui dit que le monde eft aimable, que toutes les fois qu'il s'y eft abandonné, il a goûté un plaifir réel, que toutes les fois au contraire, qui'l a voulu entrependre des actes de religion, il á reffenti

L de

the lewd father triumphing in the lewdnefs of his fons, into whofe intrigues we have known him, as eagerly and joyoufly inquifitive as if he had been in fearch of their virtues and perfections. But a letter of lewdnefs containing inftructions how to w—re with difcretion and credit, is one of thofe monfters which ftrikes us with horror at firft fight; and we can fcarce conceive more deteftation for the fon who murdered his mother, than for the father who thus murders his fon : and as none but an unnatural tyrant would have dared to perpetrate the former, fo none but a debauchee of

de la peine. Cette vive impreffion donne á un pareil homme de l'éloignement & du dé-goût pour la vertu : elle tourne fans ceffe fon ame vers ces objets que la mort va lui enlever, en forte que fans un miracle de la grace, il ne peut devenir fenfible à d'autres.

Sermons de Saurin, Tom 2. p. 397. 8, 9.

quality

SECTION VI.

quality would have profeſſedly avowed and attempted the latter. If, as the noble Lord obſerves, (reflecting on the Abbè Fenelon) no bawd could have written a more falacious letter to an innocent country girl, than the director did to his pupil; it is certain, that no pimp or pander could have wrote more falacious letters than the noble Lord has done to debauch his own ſon. We may add, upon this occaſion, that Lord Cheſterfield had little room to accuſe the Abbè of hypocriſy or diſſimulation, as ſometimes in the ſame letter, he encourages and directs the lewd amours of his ſon,* nay points out to him a particular lady as the object of criminal paſſion, and with the ſolemnity of an Apoſtle calls upon GOD to bleſs him: elſewhere

* Vol. 4. p. 230.

he beseeches him for GOD's sake to make himself master of those graces and accomplishments, which are to gain him the men, and gain him the women. And it is something remarkable, that an English fox-hunter is treated as a bear, and held out as a monster, which shocks his lordship's delicacy, and one would suspect, threatened the dissolution of his frame: but when a French w—re of figure is the game, the chace, it seems, is honourable, and the exercise such as tends to the polish and perfection of the man.

I would not charge the Noble Lord's portrait with deeper or darker colors than belong to it: I will not therefore accuse him of entertaining the principles of speculative infidelity,

not-

SECTION VI.

notwithstanding his acknowledged prejudices in favour of some eminent infidel writers. He read much; and it is not easy to reconcile a tolerable knowledge of books with a favourable opinion of infidelity; and indeed, in point of argument, his Lordship has clearly decided in favour of the Believer. Yet, in fact, Lord Chesterfield seems to have been as much a Mahometan, or a Jew, as a Christian. If we may judge of men's principles by their practice, it appears by these letters that Lord Chesterfield had no thought or concern at all about religion. Habit and practice oftner superinduce principles, or lead to no principles at all, than these operate to influence the practice. Avarice, drunkenness and other vices may frequently be observed, not founded, we believe,

lieve, in the speculative principles of infidelity, and yet inconsistent with every principle of the Christian religion. The statesman and the courtier have very strong and peculiar temptations to this practical infidelity. Charmed as his Lordship was with the honours and eclat of a court, he could not easily reconcile his passions and practice to the precepts of humility and poverty of spirit, of self-denial and self-abasement. Anxious, as he was, to please men, he could not be the servant of GOD. Admiring, as he did, the harmony of periods, the elegance of diction and the pomp of elocution, he could not well relish the natural and genuine simplicity of the gospel style. Relying, as he did, for the success of all his views and measures on human prudence and policy, we should not

SECTION VI.

not wonder, if he excluded the agency of Providence, in the conduct of human affairs. Devoted entirely, as he was, to the world, to its natural and civil advantages, we expected, as we find, that he should not bestow a thought, or extend a wish to the future, spiritual and eternal state. A courtier so spruce, so dressy, so fashionable, so anxious for his person and personal elegance, that he pretends to prescribe to the minutest circumstances in dress and deportment, could have little conception of that moral greatness, which constitutes the inner man of the heart; as the sincerity and truth in word and deed, prescribed to the scholars of the gospel, was altogether inconsistent with the versatility and duplicity, the artifice and flattery, the simulation and dissimulation, permitted and recommended as most necessary in forming the character and address of his favourite pupil. Noble, as he was, and conversant among nobles, studious of the refinements of civil policy, and the maxims of state, admitted to the persons and councils of Princes, he may be supposed to have had little relish for the foolishness of preaching, or deference to the sentiments and authority of the Carpenter's Son, and the fishermen of Galilee. His wit and delicacy must be shocked by the simplicity of their manners and maxims; and the meanness of their birth and style in life, would procure them little or no regard from the man of fashion and family. Many other causes may be assigned for Lord Chesterfield's practical infidelity, which do not at all affect the truth and reason-

able-

SECTION VI.

ableness of revelation. For instance, dulness and devotion being in his Lordship's ideas, synonimous terms; who could expect that the noble Lord should hazard his character as a wit, and renounce the applause of men, for the sake of a supreme love of GOD, in which true devotion consists, and, which is recommended as the first and leading principle by the Founder of our Christian school?

THE spirit of the gospel is so different from the spirit of the world, that it was impossible Lord Chesterfield, with all his passions and vanity about him, should enter into the kingdom of GOD, or, in other words, be a sincere and spiritual believer. Would he have given any support or authority to the cause of christianity, he should have

have been the moral man; the humble enquirer after truth; the cool and confiftent reafoner; the unprejudiced philofopher:—characters which never have been, nor ever can be united in the enemies of chriftianity. We allow him the reputation of a wit, a genius, a ftatefman and a courtier;— but in compliance with the dictates of eternal truth, we cannot allow him the honour — an honour greater than that of courtiers and kings—an honour that cometh from GOD only — the honour of being a chriftian.

LET the unbeliever, if he pleafes, enlift him in his order, and derive all the credit he can to his caufe from fo illuftrious a difciple. Chriftianity muft gain reputation and ftrength by fuch adverfaries; and the difpenfation and wifdom of GOD be only more confirmed

SECTION VI.

firmed by the vices, the vanity and folly of the men, who oppofe them. Behold the great man devoid of the principles of the chriftian religion! What, and who, is the wit, the genius, the courtier and ftatefman?—A man of univerfal complaifance, without one grain of benevolence,—affecting your confidence only in order to betray and deceive you; profeffing all languages and all knowledge, not to direct the mind and benefit mankind with ufeful difcoveries, but merely to qualify him to play a better game, and to over-reach the man he has to deal with;—a powerful fpeaker and mafter of all the graces of elocution, but applying his oratory not to promote the peace, the intereft, the honour and liberty of his country; but folely to difplay his own vanity, or to

ferve

SECTION VI.

serve the ends of a party,— fraught with a grace, or rather a gracioufnefs and overflowing courtefy to all mankind, not expreffive of any real beneficence or friendfhip towards them, but to flatter their paffions, and to render them devoted to his views;— a man of honour, yet not reftrained by any moral obligations from violating the wife or daughter of the friend who entertains him;— a genius capable of ranging through heaven and earth, to contemplate the moral and fpiritual difpenfations of GOD, ftooping his high born faculties, and confining them to a tafte for the works of art and man's device, or to the gratification of fenfes which he has in common with the brutal order;— the mighty man fubject to difeafe and diftrefs in common with the loweft of the

SECTION VI.

the people;—but as in the higheſt fortune, impious and ungrateful, ſo in the loweſt without ſupport or comfort. See here the man of taſte, the man of elegance, the man of letters, the ſenator, the orator, the patrician, the miniſter of ſtate, the counſellor of kings, when deprived of the influence, and diſcharged from the authority of religion, unſteady, fluttering, ſervile, uniform only in ſeeking the gratifications of his own paſſions; and to this end ſacrificing his time, his manhood, his honour, his truth and friendſhip, diſavowing every virtue, or diſcrediting and debaſing, by accommodating, it to ſordid and mercenary ends,—to make the fineſt figure at court, or at a ball;—to be diſtinguiſhed as the fineſt orator in the ſenate, in order to be the foremoſt in power and place; and to
improve

improve and to apply his time and talents, the beft qualities of body and mind which GOD has given him, to the intereft and advancement of his little felf. Lord Chefterfield's beft virtue is only a decent and polite vice; and it has no other ftandard or rule than the eye and opinion of the public. Its objects are pre-eminence in life: its inftruments are of the moft polifhed kind, as the moft effectual to promote the ends propofed.

THE views he entertains and conftantly holds out to his fon difcredit all the prudential advice and leffons of wifdom which may be collected from thefe letters. Confined as they are by the noble Lord to the attainment of the pleafures, the profits, the honours of our prefent precarious and
fhort

short lived existence, they are nothing more than lessons of lewdness, of avarice and ambition,—the best and most effectual means which occurred to our noble philosopher from his experience, his reading and reflections, to make you rich as the treasures, great as the titles and honours, and happy as the pleasures of this world can make you.

LET then the infidel race challenge Lord Chesterfield as their own, and what, after all, is the new subject of their triumph? A nobleman without true honour;—a senator more regardful of his own applause, than of the laws and liberty of his country;—a citizen ambitious to engross the most lucrative offices of the state; a man without feeling or friendship for his kind; a reasonable being proposing and

and purfuing as his beft and moft important good, an indulgence in pleafure, and the gratification of his groffeft paffions. Let the unbeliever fay, whether a religion, whofe fundamental principles are faith in, and a fupreme love of GOD, obedience to his laws and fubmiffion to his will: a religion which enjoins fincerity and truth in all our words and actions, calls for our benevolence to all mankind, exacts the difcharge of duty both to GOD and man upon the principles of confcience, at the expence and at the hazard of all we have. A religion which eftimating the true value and little moment of all earthly attainments, acquifitions and enjoyments, points out to our profpect a future and immortal ftate, and requires as the condition of our title to that ftate a courfe of uniform

form discipline, the practice of the social, the moral and spiritual duties. Let the unbeliever say, whether such a religion as this, does not give dignity to the lowest, and add lustre to the highest characters in life; and whether Lord Chesterfield under the influence of such a religion had not been a better man, a better citizen, a sincerer friend, a firmer patriot, a more uncorrupt senator, a more upright statesman, and a more illustrious nobleman? Such as he is, and has shewn himself, in these letters, if the infidel sect will still claim him as their own, we freely and frankly give him up, body and soul, to be made the most of, by these doctors in the minute philosophy. Let them hold out, as an example and an honour to their principles, the insinuating flatterer, the insidious fidious friend, the faithlefs gueft, the infamous pander, the betrayer of innocence and beauty, the vain orator, the venal patriot, and the ambitious ftatefman.

SECT. VII.

THOUGH appearances make against the noble Lord, yet we are willing to believe, for the honour of chriſtianity and of his Lordſhip, that he was a practical rather than a ſpeculative unbeliever, and that his commerce with this world had naturally and inſenſibly erazed out of his thoughts all taſte, all concern for, and aſpirations after a future and immortal ſtate. The man of wit, of gallantry and pleaſure, the courtier, the orator, the ſtateſman, the nobleman were the characters in which he affected to ſhine, and in which he found he moved moſt gracefully and to his advantage:

advantage: but they were characters, all which had immediate respect to this world, and which could receive no improvement from, if they did not absolutely exclude, the sublime virtues, the abstracted and spiritual graces of the christian life. His Lordship by the large share which he possessed of fame, of flattery and fortune, by the distinction of rank and title, would be less sensible of the corruption, the meanness and misery of his nature, of the need he had of a Redeemer and Sanctifier, of the authority of a superior, or of any greatness or highness more exalted than Cæsar's. The great and the noble, swimming in plenty, and accustomed to command, think it below them to seem to want, and disgraceful to obey or submit, though to the morality of
GOD

GOD himself. They must, they will be superior to the common herd of mankind, though it is in guilt and folly ; and would be as much ashamed of seeming to want any instruction from priests, from preachers, and holy enthusiasts, as they would be to be caught in an act of lewdness, or petty larceny.

THE mere man of quality is a person of the highest importance in his own and in the eyes of all about him : he is beheld at a distance with silent wonder; he is approached with submission and awful respect;—he is addressed with servility and abject flattery; he decides and dictates magisterially ; he is believed implicitly ; he is obeyed absolutely. His tone is high, his manner affected;—his smile disdainful;

ful;—his gait is flow and stately, and the whole man of a style and order that speak his superiority to the low bred vulgar. The man of quality is seen in his dress and motion. His word is law; who dare dispute it? His dictates oracular; who shall doubt or deny them? His fortune gives him all, and more than all he wants; his station commands a homage more than he is intitled to: though he may not be believed, yet all fear, all affect to fear or flatter him: he has no faults or failings, whom none dare censure or reprove. To a man thus intoxicated by his situation, and ignorant of his real state by nature, the spiritual truths and humble graces of the gospel appear strange things; and all religion is, with him, cant and enthusiasm. Who shall teach him? Who is lord over

over him? Knowing no superior on earth, he denies or forgets the GOD who is above; and will dethrone the Judge of heaven and earth, rather than submit to his tribunal. What an indignity must it be to a Peer of the Realm, to be told, that he must believe and obey, live and die, and be judged in common with other men, with his very slaves and tenants, and the lowest of the people;—that he is subject to the same law, and liable to the same condemnation; that he has not a more immortal soul, nor a better title to higher degrees of glory in a future state, than plebeians and mechanics; except from his exertion of superior virtues, moral excellencies, and higher perfections!

My Lord's habit of thinking is made

SECTION VII.

made up of quite a different set of ideas.—The refined breeding of the *beau monde*, the graces of the outward man; rank, dignity, place, pension, title;—the present state of politics; the distant prospect of things; the aspirations of the ambitious; the efforts of the factious:—camps, intrigues, battles, balls; changes and revolutions, foreign and domestic, in church and state; company and high connections; the business, the pleasure, or amusements of the day:—these so much engage *my Lord*, that he finds no leisure, need, taste or inclination for the abstracted truths, and sublime speculations of moralists and divines, —low-bred cloystered pedants, or at best respectable Hottentots, and mere barbarians in the knowledge of politeness, life and manners. He reads, if
he

he reads, in order to form his taste, to adjust and harmonize his periods, to improve and animate his eloquence, or to acquaint himself with the interests and policy of the different states and princes in Europe: but the gospel, being no ways suitable to these ends, and respecting chiefly the interest of a future and unknown world, he thinks it an unnecessary and unprofitable waste of time to spend a thought about it. The world is that ocean in which this great Leviathan takes his pastime, and leaves the prospect and provision for futurity to those vulgar souls, who have not a present and a more certain game to play. In this case, we conceive, he may not be determined by reasoning or speculative arguments, but by mere habit, by his situation

and

SECTION VII.

and connections in life, to embrace the principles of infidelity.

THE wit and the great man will preserve his favourite character in every station and circumstance of life; and unable to attend, he will celebrate and rehearse his own funeral with all the pompous solemnity of patrician greatness*. Fortune, station, nature, passion, and the world have formed in him habits and opinions as absurd and ridiculous, as if he professedly lived and died, without GOD and hope in the world.

LORD CHESTERFIELD, amidst the

---

* LORD CHESTERFIELD, a short time before his death, appeared in public in the most pompous and splendid equipage. This occasioned some surprize in the beholders, who were told by my Lord, or some of his train, that he was *rehearsing his funeral*.

natural

SECTION VII.

natural and moral ills under which he laboured affects the philosopher. It is a more pompous and sounding name than that vulgar one, a Christian. But had his lordship been influenced more by things than words, by the solidity and weight of argument more than by the appearance and vanity of science, he had not been ashamed of Christianity, the truest and sublimest philosophy that ever enlightened the sons of men; he had not lamented his being cut off from social life, and his being reduced to silence and solitude, and the condition of a lonely ghost: he had discharged the duties and supported the calamities of life with more firmness and alacrity, and he had braved the terrors of death with more decency, courage and comfort, than appeared

SECTION VII.

peared in the wit and humour affected on this folemn occafion.

WE cannot efteem highly his wifdom who rifques his whole fortune upon the chance of a card. What then fhall we think of him who throws the die for eternity with a real or affected indifference, what fhall be his portion for ever*. A fiddle and dance are

---

* THE importance of the fubject will juftify our inferting the following ferious and fenfible obfervations of M. de la Bruyere.

APRES toutes les convictions que nous devons avoir de notre religion, je ne fai comment il fe trouve des gens d'une impiete affez déterminée pour faire parade de leur irreligion au moment de la mort. Seroit-il poffible qu'ils ne fuffent éfraiez par tout ce qu'a d'affreux & de terrible cette derniere heure? Je ne puis croire malgre la feinte affurance qu'au dehors ills effaient de montrer, que leur ame foit dans une vraye tranquillité; ce calme exterieur

eft

SECTION VII.

are altogether as suitable to the character and circumstances of a dying man,

est faux, cette intrepidité trompeuse. Quand l'esprit n'auroit à soutenir que les seules frayeurs de la mort, je ne parle pas des tristes reflexions sur le passé, des suites encore plus horribles de l'avenir, il me semble que ce sqectacle doit déconcerter la plus inébranlable fermeté.

J'ai lû dans le Socrate Chrétien de Mr. de Balzac une Histoire qui me déconcerte moi même. Il dit qu'un Prince étranger étant à l'article de la mort, le theologien protestant qui avoit coûtume de prêcher devant lui, vint le visiter accompagné de deux ou trois autres de la même communion, & le conjura de faire une espece de confession de foi. Le prince lui répondit en soûriant, " Monsieur mon ami, j'ai
" bien du déplaisir de ne vous pouvoir donner le
" contentement que vous desirez de moi, vous voi-
" ez que je ne suis pas en état de faire de longs dis-
" cours : je vous dirai seulement en peu de mots que
" je crois que deux & deux font quatre, & que quatre
" & quatre font huit, Monsieur tel (montrant un
" mathematicien qui étoit là present) vous pourra
" éclaircir des autres points de notre creance."

man, as vanity and wit. The many instances of drollery and humour, which Lord Chesterfield exhibited, which he seemed to have studied in order to figure the more on his last stage, and which are handed about in pamphlets and public papers, can appear no more than a display of ill-timed foppery, and proofs of vanity and af-

N'Y-A-T,IL pas dans ces paroles quelque chose de monstreux ? Est-ce aveuglement, ou bravade d'esprit fort ? Est-ce insensibilité ou ostentation ? une homme mourir dans ces sentiments, faire gloire en mourant de croire la verité des nombres, & de n'avoir que cette creance ? Puis qu'il sait si parfaitement que " deux & deux font quatre, & que qua-" tre & quatre font huit," il aura tout le tems de calculer les années d'une éternité malheureuse.

Est-il tems de goguenarder à l'heure de la mort ? La plaisanterie peut-elle être plus hors de propos ? Avons nous oublié que c'est là le moment que dieu s'est reservé lui-même pour se railler des impies ?

M. DE LA BRUYERE, Tom. 2. p. 20.

fectation,

fectation, and remind us of the French lackey mentioned by *Rochefaucault*, who, juft before he was broke upon the wheel, entertained his fpectators with a dance upon the fcaffold erected for his execution.

MANY great characters, befides Socrates, philofophers, heroes, faints and martyrs have been diftinguifhed and recorded for their refigned deportment at this awful moment; and fome have difplayed peculiar chearfulnefs and ferenity; and not improperly; as thefe were expreffive of their peace and innocence in a caufe, which they thought the caufe of truth and God. But our noble Lord, affecting to rank among thefe heroes, unluckily begins his triumph, before the day of trial, or of battle appeared. His triumph was therefore premature and impertinent.

The

SECTION VII.

The philosopher, the hero, and the martyr suffered an unjust, an unnatural or extraordinary death. Their arguments, therefore, and their elevation of soul under such sufferings, the more raise our attention, admiration and applause. But the Lord Chesterfield's natural death, amidst peace and plenty, honour and reputation required no extraordinary effort to support it. His figuring therefore, upon this occasion, and indifference expressed for what shall become of him for ever, is mere rant and extravagance,—a vain and wanton ferocity, unsupported by any rational and religious motives, and which the author would have to pass for the dictates of calm philosophy. *

LORD

---

* THE following Anecdote communicated to the Author by a person of the first eminence in the Church,

and

SECTION VII.

Lord Chesterfield had sagacity enough to see and lament the errors of

and distinguished by his candor and humanity, may serve to shew that Lord Chesterfield did not always entertain the same hardy sentiments and epicurean indifference in respect to death and its consequences which he has expressed in these Letters.

"About eight years ago, he was seized with a sickness at his stomach, and a violent flux, which continuing to resist medicine had so far weakened him, that it was thought by his friends, and he himself expected, that he should live but a few hours. I visited him in his chamber, and with his usual appearance of pleasantry and good humour, he told me that he should be brought to return my visit next week, and to receive the last office of my friendship. I thought this a fair opportunity for some serious conversation with him, which I introduced by expressing a satisfaction, that feeble as he was in body, he could look on his approaching dissolution with so much ease and complacency. He saw my drift, and gave way to it. I do not remember that he expresly professed himself to be a Christian, but in many respects he talked much like one; he spoke largely of his confidence in God's mercy and good-of the human mind, and he had senfibility enough to feel and acknowledge the calamities incident to human nature; but he had not greatness of mind enough to accept the humble and healing truths of the gospel, peculiarly suited to assist mankind in supporting and improving those calamities, and in chasing away those errors. The gospel, though the dictate and manifestation of eternal truth, must naturally revolt the noble Lord, when

ness; and I perfectly remember his conclusion was, I know it is my duty to submit my will in all things to the will of God. I do so entirely, and my understanding also, as far as I am able."

After doing this justice to the noble Lord, and answering, as we conceive, the benevolent views of the communicator of this anecdote, we cannot but add, that resignation in distress to the God of nature, or a faith that carries us no further than our reason approves, is not the faith or resignation of a Christian.

it

it would reduce him to the character of a miserable sinner, or humble and contrite penitent. The graces of the spirit would be laughed at, if recommended to the man who admired — singularly admired the graces of the dancing-master, or who made all the graces center in a dancing-master. Neither Jesus, nor his disciples were polite, well-bred gentlemen, from whom you might learn the art of pleasing men — the air of a court or the address of a courtier.

"Blessed are the meek, — blessed
" are the poor in spirit,—blessed are the
" pure in heart,—blessed are they who
" do hunger and thirst after righteous-
" ness," are moralities of so meagre, so mean, and humble an aspect, that they might become a cell, a cottage, or a cloyster, but could never be in-

tended for the use, or enter into the practice of the man of the world, the man of wit, the man of gallantry and fashion. Noble blood resents the affront offered it in imposing such trite, such thread-bare, such illiberal stuff, — the dreams of platonic madmen — hot-brained enthusiasts and ghostly impostors, upon the modern gentile world. Brotherly love and charity are vulgar antiquated terms, in the room of which the Noble Lord has substituted insinuation, address, adulation, attention, assiduities, and all the external graces of a studied complaisance. Lord Chesterfield was evidently a man of this world; the wisdom of GOD therefore in revealing, and directing our views to another, must be no better than foolishness in the estimation of his Lordship.

It

SECTION VII.

It is well that Lord Chesterfield has given us all his heart; we thence learn, as we have before observed, how poor and miserable, how blind and naked, is human nature, animated with wit and genius, polished by education, improved by reason and reflection, and refined by courtly manners, without the influence and advantage of religion. We see wit evaporating in vanity; genius and eloquence terminating in ambition; the passions degenerating into lewdness; wisdom confined to human policy and intrigue; good faith and good conscience supplanted by profession and outward seeming; benevolence banished by good manners; friendship by complaisance; sincere virtue and a steady faith by self-love and a prudential philosophy; and all the devoirs of life, respecting what we owe to GOD and man, contracted to the narrow view of pleafing and gratifying Self.

Let us fuppofe Lord Chefterfield had admitted Chriftianity to influence his faith and practice: had he been lefs honourable, or deemed fuch, by his fubjection to the Almighty? Had he been lefs happy under the protection, the order, and guidance of an all-wife and all gracious Providence, than as fubject to fortune, chance, or nature? Had not fincerity, opennefs of manners, and cordial chriftian benevolence, contributed as eafily, and effectually, to eftablifh his character in the world, and conciliate the love of mankind, as artificial addrefs, diffembled friendfhip, and French grimace? Had his Lordfhip's name at this day been held lefs facred, or had he been lefs refpectable in the eyes of his King and
Country

SECTION VII. 183

Country—had he been known to have served both from principles of loyalty and love, not from motives of interest and ambition? Had his Lordship's prudence been arraigned, if he had added to the wisdom of the serpent, the innocence of the dove; or if he had improved and applied those excellent rules he has given us for the improvement of our time, regularity and diligence in business, to more extensive views than those which are confined to the bounds of mortality? Had the Noble Lord been less a moralist, had he, instead of inflaming the passions, and prompting to licentious pleasures, endeavoured to correct the malignity, and eradicate the depravity of human nature? Had he been less a philosopher, had he taken in GOD as a necessary agent in the process of nature, and favoured us and himself with some rational, if not pious, reflections, on his infinite providence and perfections? Had his Lordship's genius, or literature, been discredited by their being employed in recommending to mankind in general, and to his son in particular, the love of virtue, of glory, and immortality? Had the noble Lord departed from his dignity, in acknowledging himself subject to the Lord of heaven and earth, an imitator of divine perfection, and an aspirer after the eternal existence and happiness of the celestial orders? Do we not see a meanness and degradation in the Noble Lord's spirit and character, when we observe him a mere man of this world, a mere animal, and like his fellow-animals, providing for no more than his present being

SECTION VII.

being, without an eye lift up to heaven, or a thought for his future exiftence ? *Poor human nature!* we will fay with his Lordfhip—poor, yet proud, proud of its nothingnefs, of its feathers, its ribbands, and rattles—of its errors, ignorance, and blindnefs — proud of the popular breath, of the fmiles of a court, and the promifes of a courtier; of deceiving and being deceived — of living to vanity and lies—the dream of the day—the fhadow of a momentary exiftence:—Whilft we are afraid or afhamed of acknowledging our wants, would be thought great and honourable, wife and knowing, happy and independent, rich, abounding in all things and wanting nothing; and to conceal our poverty and nakednefs, would renounce the bounty, and reject the bleffings of heaven itfelf.

We

We really pity the Noble Lord, labouring under diftrefs, yet above feeking any help, or entertaining any hope from heaven; a feeble mortal, yet independent of his Maker; helplefs, yet renouncing or foregoing all helps from the Almighty;—without comfort in life, and, what is ftill worfe, without comfort or profpect in death, and making our very infirmities, which fhould be the fubject of humiliation, motives to prayer, and recommend to us a Redeemer and Deliverer, a kind of apology for, and juftification of all the pride, the follies, the vices, the inconfiftencies, and extravagancies of human nature.

WE cannot help fmiling at his Lordfhip's French hafh of complaifance and good manners, which he would

prefent

SECTION VII.

present us with in the room of the old fashioned English repast, good faith and a good conscience: but we are really inclined to pity the Noble Lord, when amidst the distresses of nature, upon the appearance of his dissolution, we find him ignorant, or, in support of his pride, affecting to be ignorant, that there is a GOD above him, or that he has an immortal soul: we lament the weakness of human nature, when we observe the Noble Lord, with honours and titles thus mean, with fortune thus poor, with wit thus ridiculous, with reason and philosophy so deficient in knowledge, and the art of ordinary computation.

POOR human nature! conscious of, yet ashamed to acknowledge its wants; and though a beggar, too proud to ask

ask assistance of the Supreme Lord of Heaven and Earth. Miserable condition of mortality, when uninfluenced and unsupported by the principles and power of religion! To be weary of a silly world, sensible of the wretched bargain of life; to feel the *fragment of his wretched carcase, and the timbers of his crazy vessel* running down to decay, yet, careless of consequences and without hope and prospect of repair or reparation, speaks a degeneracy which a heathen philosopher would have been ashamed of;—a pride which nature shrinks from and abhors, and which decency and common sense, reason, as well as revelation, condemn. Socrates and Seneca act the proper part, stand forth like heroes, and disgrace that affected insensibility and indifference, that submission to nature and

its

its laws, to any thing, or nothing, after death, expressed by the Noble Lord, on this solemn subject.

May we not suppose the truth to have been this? That the Noble Lord affected to figure as a wit, an orator, and a Peer of Great Britain: and supposing this world to be the whole of human existence, he possessed his share of fame and fortune, and with this he was content; and as he did not naturally relish, he could not easily admit a future state, wherein moral and spiritual distinctions only would have place, would advance to superior degrees of honour and happiness, and where a Peer of Great Britain might possibly rank below peasants and slaves.

We wish that these letters had afforded

SECTION VII.

forded us an occasion of exhibiting the Noble Lord in a more amiable, more exalted, and more splendid, that is, in a more Christian light;—a wit decent and chastised, an orator spirited in the display, and powerful in the recommendation of truth and virtue; a patriot steady and brave, in promoting the benefit, and asserting the rights and liberties of his country; the man open, sincere, and benevolent; kind, yet firm; placid, yet resolute; acting, and acted by convictions of conscience;—animated and elevated by the principles of divine truth, by faith in the present GOD, and the prospect of his future kingdom and glory, and exalted and transformed by divine love and heavenly hope to a greatness and dignity, a splendour and love, beyond all that

Kings,

SECTION VII.

Kings, and courts of Kings, can exhibit and beſtow.

But happy it is for mankind, that the eternal truth of GOD is fixed, is uniform and unchangeable; without this, we may obſerve, to what various opinions, abſurdities, and immoral principles; miſled by the infirmity of nature, the influence of paſſion, the vanity of wit, the oſtentation of ſcience, the conjectures of reaſon, the authority of great names, we muſt be expoſed. GOD, and his truth, reſpect not the diſtinctions of perſons and characters in life; great and little, high and low, are equally ſubject to the authority of the Almighty: his favour and acceptance are equally and equitably promiſed to all thoſe who love and obey him. The wit and the

Peer

Peer of Great Britain are regarded as mere moral agents in the eye of the Holy and All-perfect GOD: and human dignities, and diftinctions, titles, and names of honour, muft be confidered by the high and Holy One, who inhabiteth eternity, as the affects of our finful pride, the characteriftics of our vanity, of our meannefs, and littlenefs. The humble, the devout, the good heart, is what alone can recommend us to the regards of our Maker. Wits are feathers, and nobles more contemptible than flaves, when they intrench upon the prerogatives, and affect to be like or above the Moft High.

THE truly great and refpectable in the eye of GOD, by the rule and law of reafon, is he who from a confcioufnefs

SECTION VII.

oufnefs of his weaknefs, his worthleffnefs and nothingnefs, humbles himfelf in the duft before the throne of the Almighty, accepts and obeys his truth however made known to him, refigns himfelf to his Providence, cooperates with him in promoting the happinefs of mankind, and from a conviction of the vanity of a paffing life, extends his views, and builds his hopes on a future and immortal ftate. Void of fuch a rational and moral conduct as this, the richeft among mankind are but beggars, the wifeft, are but fools, and the nobleft mean and degenerate — the phantoms of a day, the mock-heroes of a ftage, trembling under their ftep, and haftening every moment to a ruin. The greateft, diftinguifhed by titles, by offices and honours, by opulence by luxury,

SECTION VII.

luxury, by splendour and equipage, eminent for wit, for taste, for literary accomplishments, and every external advantage of life, but ignorant of, indifferent to, or despisers of sacred truth, and of the relation they stand in to GOD its author, in the eye of reason are without real dignity and honour; without security, steadiness or a proper relish of the best fortune, without support or comfort in the worst; slaves to sense and passion; blind to the beauties and glories of GOD in his works of Creation and Providence, uninformed by immortal truth, unanimated by any immortal prospect, unacquainted with peace of conscience, strangers to the exalted delight of communion with GOD by devotion and prayer, and hurrying down the precipice of life with the gloomy expectation of perishing for ever.

WHAT

SECTION VII.

WHAT dignity of sentiment or character can we expect or admire in such a conduct as this? Without principle or virtue the hero is a murderer, the statesman a stock-jobber, and the first peer of the realm only the most illustrious plunderer. Without principle and virtue prudence is but cunning, and wisdom short-sighted artifice; wit is licentious, and good manners are insidious; complaisance is hypocrisy, and profession of friendship treachery; splendour is a painted cloud; power a raging tempest; riches a sordid mass; nobility a shining but pestilential meteor; and all the distinguished eminence and valuable possessions of man, no better than the flower, or flowery dream of yesterday.

SECT. VIII.

UPON a free and impartial review of Lord Chesterfield's Letters, you see what a poor and contemptible figure the noble Lord makes, as a Moralist and a Patriot; as a Father, a Senator or a Briton. To give his readers a hearty detestation of the principles and practices recommended in his letters; and to confirm them in the antiquated principles of virtue and religion, let us exhibit the out-lines and some of the striking features of that genuine and manly virtue which was adopted, practised and recommended by the patriots and sages of ancient Greece and Rome — was taught in their schools, was maintained in the forum,

SECTION VIII.

forum, and afserted in the senate; was incorporated with their laws, inspired the love of liberty, and animated the several orders of the state to do and suffer all things for the happiness and glory of their country.

VIRTUE would one of those sages have said, consists not in verbal trifling, in formal definitions, in school distinctions, and in the subtle refinements of metaphysical or political sophists * : but it is a divine ardor of the soul

---

* IN a quotation from Baron *Montesquieu* made by Lord Chesterfield for the use of his son, it is said, " In monarchies the principal branch of education " is not taught in colleges or academies. — The " virtues we are taught here, are less what we owe, " to others, than to ourselves; they are not so much " what draws us towards society, as what distin- " guishes us from our fellow-citizens. Here the ac- " tions

foul better felt than defined or defcribed, warming the heart, engaging the paffions,

" tions of men are judged not as virtuous, but as
" fhining ; not as juft but as great, not as reafon-
" able but as extraordinary. When honour here
" meets with any thing noble in our actions, it is
" either a judge that approves them, or a fophifter
" by whom they are excufed.

"It allows of gallantry, when united with the
" idea of fenfible affection, or with that of con-
" queft : — it allows of cunning and craft, when
" joined with the notion of greatnefs of foul, or im-
" portance of affairs ; as for inftance, in politics,
" with whofe fineffes it is far from being offended.
" It does not forbid adulation, but when feparate
" from the idea of a large fortune, and connected
" only with the fenfe of our mean condition.——

"Truth in converfation is here a neceffary point.
" But is it for the fake of truth? By no means.
" Truth is requifite only, becaufe a perfon habitu-
" ated to veracity has an air of boldnefs and free-
" dom.—In proportion as this kind of franknefs is
" commended that of the common people is defpifed,
" which

SECTION VIII.

paſſions, captivating the affections, informing and charming the whole man into a love of truth and honour, of GOD and goodneſs, and animating him with a ſpirit and fortitude to do and

" which has nothing but truth and ſimplicity for its
" object.—The education of monarchies requires
" a certain politeneſs of behaviour.—But polite-
" neſs, generally ſpeaking, does not derive its ori-
" ginal from ſo pure a ſource. It riſes from a de-
" ſire of diſtinguiſhing ourſelves. It is pride that
" renders us polite: we are flattered with being
" taken notice of for a behaviour that ſhews we are
" not of a mean condition.———

" A COURT air conſiſts in quitting a real for a
" borrowed greatneſs. The latter pleaſes the courtier
" more than the former.—At court we find a delica-
" cy of taſte in every thing, a delicacy ariſing from
" the conſtant uſe of the ſuperfluities of life, from
" the variety, and eſpecially the ſatiety of pleaſures,
" from the multitude, and confuſion of fancies,
" which, if they are but agreeable, are ſure of be-
" ing well received.—Here it is that honour inter-

" feres

SECTION VIII.

and suffer all things, in the prosecution of his favourite objects, which alone he affects and aspires after, though at the expence of his ease, his pleasure, his interest, his reputation, or even of life itself.

Least of all has selfishness any connection with virtue, and is the meanest and most infamous principle that was ever assigned or recommended as a motive to the conduct of rational beings: for what are avarice and ambition, fraud and rapine, hypocrisy and

" feres with every thing;—to this whimsical ho-
" nour it is owing that the virtues are only just
" what it pleases; it adds rules of its own invention
" to every thing prescribed to us; it extends or li-
" mits our duties according to its own fancy, whe-
" ther they proceed from religion, politics, or mo-
" rality."

Ld. Chesterfield's Let. Vol. 3, p. 32, &c.

SECTION VIII.

and flattery, corruption and bribery, gaming, luxury and lewdnefs, with all the fopperies, follies, vanities and vices in fafhion, but the effects of that felfifhnefs, which Lord Chefterfield has recommended as the ruling principle of his fon's conduct.

VIRTUE — would Socrates and his followers, would Cicero, Seneca, and Antonine, would Livy and Cato have faid; — virtue is an immortal principle, which came down from heaven, and points to heaven : it is immutable as well as immortal : it is the conftitution of GOD in nature, and recommended by every motive, that fhould influence a rational being. It is equally binding at all times, and in all places ; upon all orders and degrees of men ; upon mafters and flaves, upon on subjects and sovereigns. It stamps dignity upon the lowest, and bestows the only true honour upon the highest characters in human nature. Its intrinsic excellence disdains all artificial appearances, or external ornaments. Without it princes are the mockery of majesty, nobles are plebeians; and with it plebeians tread on the necks of nobles.

Virtue belongs to no peculiar station or character in life. It is the duty, the ornament, the happiness, the honour of every reasonable being. It is of the same value, power and dignity in a prison as in a palace, in a cottage as on a throne. It is only distinguished by the opposition it meets with, by the pains and penalties it undergoes, by the pleasure it resists,

by

by the paffions it conquers, and by the falfe glory it defpifes. It feeks no ample theatre for its difplay, nor the trumpet of fame to report its praifes to the world; but is content with the plaudit of confcience and the approbation of heaven. Virtue is independent of fortune and honours, of place or titles: it is often richeft in poverty and great in its humility, it rifes by oppofition, and fhines moft illuftrious in the fhade. It is more vigorous than wit, — more lovely than beauty, more auguft than power; more beneficent, more pleafing than juftice; more arduous, more enterprifing and fublimer than ambition. It is powerful without friends, fatisfied without fortune, and great in its contempt of, and fuperiority to the world. It affects neither plenty nor want, but

content

content with the difcharge of duty, leaves the perquifites of office to others. It affects no ftate or pomp. It is mighty in its own ftrength; magnificent in its own greatnefs; without gold or purple, fhines by its own native fplendour, and is a conqueror without the eclat of a triumph.

VIRTUE is decent, modeft and retired, except when confcience calls it forth, and duty pufhes it forward to a more arduous and public exertion. It labours, though filent, yet unwearied; preferving though oppofed, and fpirited though depreffed or neglected. Watered, foftered, and refrefhed by the dews of heaven, it grows and flourifhes though unheeded; and is abundant in precious fruits
regard-

SECTION VIII.

regardlefs of the ungrateful hand that gathers them.

VIRTUE, genuine virtue feeks no favour, but that of heaven; refpects no eye, but that of GOD. It confiders the loweft ftation, as the appointment of Providence, and a fphere ample enough for the difplay of its prowefs: and it annexes true honour and happinefs, only to the faithful difcharge of duty and confcience. Virtue, if it cannot command, is content to deferve fuccefs, and is fatisfied with the loweft place, as the place of honour, where it minifters to duty, and affords a fubject of patience and magnanimity, in doing and fuffering the will of GOD.

VIRTUE would confider as the greateft

greatest insult, and the foulest diminution of its honour, the bribe of avarice and ambition,—the temptation to luxury and lewdness, as the price of its conduct and concurrence, in any measure proposed, or duty exacted. It is delicately sensible of any approach to vice, though gilded with the fairest appearance, and recommended by the most splendid examples. Secrecy itself would not tempt it to betray a trust; to an infraction of faith, or to violate its sanctity, though heaven and earth could be supposed asleep, or to connive at the violation. Virtue is superior to dejection and fear: conscious of its own intentions and sincerity, it is not anxious to please, or fearful to offend. Satisfied in a good conscience, and of having given no just cause of offence, it bears

SECTION VIII.

bears no ill will,—it apprehends no injury, nor ſtands in awe of the frown of a ſuperior. It knows no ſuperiority, it reſpects no power, it reveres no greatneſs, it adores no divinity but what is founded in moral excellence, and ſuperior goodneſs. It reverences the honeſt ſlave above the flagitious Peer or Prince. Virtue is hardy to enterprize, and vigorous to perſevere; is neither damped by the neglect of the great, nor moved by the contempt and reproaches of the world. It heſitates not at doubts and difficulties, nor is timid and cautious of daring danger or incurring cenſures. It advances wherever duty calls, and would rather run the hazard of a defeat, than be wanting in the proſecution of a brave and honeſt attempt. It betrays no ſervile fear, nor is practiſed in a
ſtudied

studied and laboured complaisance. Virtue fears none but GOD, and acknowledges no authority but that of heaven. It receives no direction but from the Divine Will, and knows no dependence but on the Divine Power. It is of too strong a habit, and of too masculine a complexion to stoop to the delicacies of fashionable life, or to the prescribed forms of polite address, and artful insinuation. Superior to flattery as to falshood, it is constant to the truth: it looks, it speaks, it acts the dictates of the heart: unbyassed by fear or favour, unbroken by pleasure or pain, by the effects of prosperous or adverse fortune; it contends for the truth with a simplicity, sincerity and ardour that do honour to the cause; and would rather lose than gain an advantage by any indirect methods of of profecuting and promoting it. Virtue is fuperior to injuries and affronts: confcious of its own native ftrength, it is unhurt by the one, and defpifes the other. It were not virtue that fhould depend for its exiftence and exercife on the good will or malice of others. It were no temple facred to, and inhabited by the divinity of truth and virtue, that fhould fuffer violation from the falfhood, the injuftice and impiety of men. The out-works may be defaced or demolifhed, but true virtue, the divinity of the place, is and muft be for ever inviolable, unaffailable, unimpaired and impregnable againft every attempt that may be made againft its firmnefs and compact conftruction. Virtue is a ftranger to repulfe and difgrace. Its very efforts are honourable, where they meet not with succefs; it is even the more diſtinguiſhed by diſappointment, and riſes more illuſtrious from a fall. Beggared, baniſhed, diſgraced and tortured, it is ſtill virtue; and the more ſo from the fortune, the diſgrace, the baniſhment and beggary it undergoes.

VIRTUE is the repreſentative and ſubſtitute of GOD in the ſoul of man. It ſupports, it confirms, it ſtrengthens, it ſanctifies, it exalts him above the frailties of nature, and the terrors of mortality. It gives him a power invincible, a ſtrength invulnerable, a peace inviolable, a faith immoveable, hopes immortal, and a ſpirit infinite and incompreſſible.

VIRTUE is the only ennobling quality-

SECTION VIII.

lity, the only nobility in nature. Artificial nobility, the creation of mere policy or power, and conferred on the vicious, the venal and the base has no name or place in the temple of honour. It is the great soul alone, the heroic action, or the beneficent deed, that speaks the great man, and transfers his name with honour to future ages. The eminently virtuous, though proscribed by power, and damned by the voice of the senate and people, challenge the first honours of the state, and are entitled to the most lasting memory in the records of fame; while the vain and ambitious, the public pillager, the betrayer of his friends and country, every corrupt dependent on a court, though distinguished by the most splendid titles and offices, which imperial favour can bestow, are exposed to the curse of the present, and doomed to oblivion, or to the just reproaches of all future ages. Virtue adopts as her sons of honour the humbly good, and makes a contempt of fame the best title to fame. Virtue admits no blood for patrician, which is tainted with ignorance or folly, pride or passion, with voice or corruption. Virtue confers the coronet, a crown and kingdom, on him alone who is master of himself, who conquers his passions, who beholds with an undazzled eye superfluous riches, superficial honours, and empty titles, the blandishments of false pleasure, and the eclat of false glory.

A FAILURE in virtue is a forfeiture of title: a character debased and inverted is more conspicuously infamous; and

SECTION VIII.

and the nobleman descending to the low arts, the vile practices, and corrupt manners of base and vulgar souls, in departing from his proper character, forfeits his dignity and title in life, and renders himself an object of superior scorn, and more deserved contempt. Great names and illustrious titles, distinguished by corruption, by degeneracy and licentiousness in principle and practice, exhibit a peculiar malignity; as the sun and stars converted into blood would strike us only as more signal and horrible portents. When Princes commence tyrants, and Nobles degenerate into servile sycophants, or modish debauchees, virtue razes their names from the records of time, or damns them with immortal infamy.

SECTION VIII.

Virtue, if it is severe and awful as the GOD who inspires it, is like him just, benevolent, and altogether lovely. Sincere in its views, and upright in its intentions, it has nothing to fear or to conceal; and, secure in a good conscience, it disdains all servility or flattery, or any indirect means to attain its end, and carry its views into execution. It is generally happy in the effects it produces, as it is honest in the means it employs. Sincere virtue commands the esteem and confidence of all who deserve it; while complaisance only attempts to ensnare the credulity of those upon whom it is practised. The plainness and simplicity of the language of virtue speaks its sincerity and veracity; while the courtier's studied phrase, profession of compliment, and voluminous expression

SECTION VIII.

sion of kindness, justly render him suspected. The benevolence of virtue is seen by deeds, not by words. The delicacy of feeling is heightened by the perfection of virtue; and the sensibility of nature is improved by its purity. The most virtuous have always been the most compassionate, the most ready to instruct and to inform, to give and to forgive: they content not themselves with verbal condolence, and affected sympathy, but shew their good will by honest advice, by friendly remonstrances, and by real benefits procured or conferred on the unhappy. Virtue is not confined by selfish or partial considerations; it embraces the whole human race as the object of its attention and compassion; and seconds the pretensions, and promotes the interest, of all who have a claim to humanity, or wear a kindred form.

VIRTUE spurns, with high disdain, the official bribe and mercenary pension, and seeks not its own, but the good of others. — The dignity, the glory, the very essence of virtue consists in its disinterestedness; — avarice, vanity and ambition, lewdness, luxury, passions of the selfish order, true virtue despises and abhors. The highest instance of self-denial speaks the sublimest efforts of virtue, which, if it seeks its own good, seeks it as the effect or consequence, not as the motive of duty; — or, seeks it as a moral good, consisting in the delight of doing good, and the complacency of conscience in the approbation of heaven.

TRUE

SECTION VIII.

TRUE virtue co-operates with the order of Providence and the divine difpenfations; promoting as it is able, the advantage of all; and would deem as facrilege any advantage procured at the expence, and to the damage of others. Virtue is the pureft emanation and image of the Divinity, that can inform the human foul: and the moral qualities it difplays, truth, righteoufnefs, goodnefs, mercy are the beft refemblance of the moral attributes of GOD. Virtue like its great author and infpirer, is fteady, immoveable and uniform, of a rectitude inviolable, of a benignity, or at leaft of a benevolence inexhauftible, and happy in proportion to its power of communicating happinefs to others. Virtue, in the moral, like the fun in the natural world, is not weary, nor wanders in its courfe, but fheds its benign influence through the whole fyftem; and though clouds and tempefts may for a time weaken its power, and obfcure its luftre, it perfeveres in its fteady courfe, with light and fplendor unimpaired.

But virtue is fairer and more lovely than fun and ftars: thefe act not, but are acted by a natural procefs and a neceffary order. Virtue is the order of choice, the procefs of reafon and liberty, and amidft oppofing enemies and contending paffions acquits itfelf a conqueror: unfuccefsful as it may be in its efforts, and fometimes defeated in its views, depreffed by violence, blackned by calumny, buried in the fhade, or deformed by calamity, it is ftill auguft: and, like beauty and innocence

SECTION VIII.

nocence in tears, more lovely and affecting than the high born proftitute adorned with all the glitter of wealth, the delicacy of drefs and the pomp of equipage. It is a divine vigour in the foul, triumphing over the darknefs, the mifery and ills of nature, and converting them into objects of acquiefcence, complacency and tranquillity. Virtue is the image of GOD ftamped upon human nature, refining its bafenefs, exalting its meannefs, enlightening its darknefs, enlarging its littlenefs, enriching its poverty, healing its maladies, and converting its very wants, diftreffes and miferies into abundance, into triumph, into happinefs and glory. Poor human nature indeed without this divine treafure! Amidft opulence how needy; amidft titles and honours how ignoble and mean,

mean, in a palace how miserable, how contemptible on a throne!

True virtue by its self-abasement, self-denial, and renunciation of self, gains universal admirers. It respects the public as the best good, and truth as the most valuable possession: in their support and defence, with Phocion and Socrates, it is careless of life and fortune, and nobly embraces poverty and death. Virtue renounces all selfish and sensual enjoyments, and adopts the social and moral, as the truest and only happiness; and raised above all low and vulgar prejudices and passions, it considers the cause of truth and the cause of GOD as the same, which it defends at the hazard of its being.—Yet though bold and daring to the death, virtue the child of heaven
wears

wears an angel's fmile, and is diftinguifhed by all the graces of its divine original : elevated and afpiring, yet winning and attractive; benevolent, gracious, courteous and condefcending; its features formed to complacency, its voice attuned to harmony; its eye beaming with benignity; and all its motions, though compofed and fteady, yet graceful, elegant and unaffuming; modeft without affectation, engaging without art, pleafing without defign or flattery, and commanding friends and admirers by a fimplicity that is above all art and difguife. Virtue, though retired, has nothing to difguife or be afhamed of;—is open, generous and unembarraffed upon every occafion; though humble and unaffuming in its garb, afpect and addrefs, it is manly and fpirited in its

conduct

conduct, and displays a fortitude unsubmitting and unappalled in the discharge of duty.

VIRTUE is a steady and inflexible principle, and depends not on the accidents of time and place, or on the fashion of the world: it surveys the progressive rise and fall of states, of nations and empires, with the short-lived existence, and certain and universal mortality of the human race; and under this conviction aspires to a name, a character and exstience, which will mock the flight of ages, and survive the desolations of nature. While the courtier flutters the shining insect of the day, virtue erects for her sons a temple sacred to immortality. The good man apprehends no death or dissolution! invited to heaven and called

to

SECTION VIII. 223

to glory and immortality, he foars above this dim spot which men call earth, and is loft in the boundlefs, the infinite, the incomprehenfible progreffion of eternity that appears to his profpect.

YET virtue, though coloured with all the graces of heaven, has no charms or beauty, were the faculties are indifpofed to receive or relifh it; and we wonder not to hear chriftians called enthufiafts, or platonic madmen, when they exhibit GOD and virtue in colours too bright, and in a form too exalted for the tafte of the fenfual epicurean philofopher. Virtue among fome of the ancients was painted an auguft figure *; her countenance

*Και φαηναι αυτω δυο γυναικας προιεναι μεγαλας, και την μεν ετεραν ευπρεπη τε ιδειν και ελευθεριον, φυσει

κε-

224 SECTION VIII.

tenance open; amiable and elevated, with an air of conscious dignity, and her person adorned with native elegance; her look with modesty, every gesture with decency, and her garments altogether of the purest white: but we would convert the celestial Seraph into an errant strumpet, in order to suit our taste and gratify our passions. How lovely, how attractive is she in her native charms, her divine beauty and happy effects! The founder of cities, the enacter of laws, — the support of society, the health of a state, the conqueror in war, the ornament in peace; — the source of national order and hppiness, the security of property, the cement of

κεκοσμημενην το μεν σωμα καθαροτητι, τα δε ομματα αιδοι, το δε σχημα σωφροσυνη, εσθητι δε λευκη.

XENOPHON MEM. SOCR.

friend-

SECTION VIII.

friendship,—the bond of conjugal fidelity, the parent of domestic harmony; the peasant's inviolable tenure; the hermit's whispering angel,—the proscribed patriot's, the dying philosopher's and heroe's support and comfort! Virtue the bliss of private life; the best defence, ornament and honour of public characters;—the beauty of youth, the stay of old age,—the subject's unalienable right, and to the Prince a security stronger than that of a crown! Virtue the fairest flower that opens upon earth, the sweetest incense, that ascends the skies!

Such was virtue in the estimation of ancient wisdom; and for what are we, according to modern manners, to exchange this inestimable jewel!— For a place, a title, or a wh—re! Shall this virtue, the divine image and effulgence,

effulgence, the imprefs of the divinity upon the human form, the only refemblance of man to his maker; fhall this virtue be at the mercy of paffion and prejudice, of vice and folly; of Lords or Commons, of Priefts or Princes, to model it according to their own intereft, ambition or avarice? Virtue is a robe of heavenly woof and texture, which will not admit any fhape or form which human invention, folly or fafhion fhall give it. Let the Prince command his fubjects! Let the patrician lord it over his flaves! But let not either of them prefume to dictate to the Lord of heaven and earth; Shall the immutable law of GOD,—the law of nature and reafon be relaxed, altered or abrogated at the will of a frail, a blind and corrupt mortal? Or has a peer of Great Britain any more authority to cancel the

consti-

SECTION VIII.

conſtitution of the moral, than of the natural world? The ſame right which the Lord Cheſterfield has to recommend whoredom and adultery, any other man has to recommend and practiſe calumny, pillage public or private, perjury, murder, or any other ſpecies of corruption and villainy, to which human nature may be inclined.

MAY we preſume to ſuppoſe that there is any political malevolence in the great, in thus attempting to traduce virtue, and to deſtroy its exiſtence out of the world?— That this principle which raiſes the loweſt, enriches the pooreſt, and ennobles the meaneſt, which renders every man great and independent, or dependent on heaven alone, being extinguiſhed, titles and fortune, offices and honours might rear their heads aloft, and, as the only valuable diſtinctions, challenge the univerſal homage of mankind? Such degeneracy, ſuch impious artifice, can ſurely never lodge in any polite breaſt; and we ſhould rather ſuppoſe in the caſe before us, that the noble Lord's principles were the effect of his education, not ſufficiently inured to virtue,—or of his good fortune, not checked by any ſignal diſtreſs or calamity,—or of his temper and conſtitution diſpoſed to pleaſure, vanity and wit,—or of the applauſe which the laſt gained him, and that general good reputation he held among mankind;—all which might tend to hide his infirmities from himſelf, and from the inſpection of others, to whom he laid himſelf not ſo open, as he has done in this confidential correſpondence with his ſon.

What-

SECTION VIII.

WHATEVER was the ground of his principles, it is to be lamented for his own sake, for the sake of his friends and of his country, that they were ever published to the world: they are indeed in no degree dangerous from any plausible reasons, or speculative arguments by which he attempts to support them: but the very name and * example of so accomplished a Nobleman, may have a very unhappy effect upon the morals of Britons:—and we have only to wish as a counter-balance or counter-ferment to the poison which these letters convey, that a patrician or patricians of the first name,

* UNUM exemplum aut luxuriæ aut avaritiæ multum mali facit: convictor delicatus paullatim enervat & emollit: malignus comes quamvis candido & simplici, rubiginem suam affricuit.

SENEC. EP. 7-

distinguished as much by their virtues as by their titles, revered for their reverence to the Almighty, and exalted above others for their superior love to GOD and man, would stand forth in the cause of truth and virtue, and by their writings, as well as their example, rescue morality from the violation it has suffered, and still suffers from the wanton and licentious pen of Lord Chesterfield.

A PATRICIAN thus engaged, would do himself the highest honour, and add to his other titles that of saviour of his country. A patrician supporting its laws, promoting or restoring its virtue, combating its worst enemies, and exterminating principles, which have upon tryal proved, and must for ever prove most fatal to the
security

SECTION VIII.

security, the stability, the liberty, the happiness and grandeur of states and empires;—a patrician thus engaged, would be more than noble; we should hail him as divine—a legate commissioned by heaven, to vindicate the laws of heaven, to deliver mankind from meanness, corruption and misery, from false pleasure, false delicacy, false honour, and false greatness, to invite the wanderer into the path that leads to the truest relish of his being, and to the sovereign happiness and glory of his nature.

Nobles are not wanting, qualified by their learning to explain, and by their eloquence to defend and enforce the laws and liberties of their country;—and we see in the instance before us, a nobleman distinguishing him-

SECTION VIII.

himself by his abilities, and powerful and persuasive in the art of seduction and vice. And shall no genius, no patrician, no orator appear in defence of the first and the best cause, the cause of injured truth and declining virtue?—a cause more important to the interest of the British empire, than all her taxes, all her colonies and all her treasures;—a cause with the decline of which must decline the industry, the temperance, the courage, the honour and reputation, the internal order and prosperity, and the external enlargement and grandeur of the state;—a cause which GOD and nature have published, and still publish to the world, and which therefore renders our contempt of it the more impious, and our neglect of it the more inexcusable!

SECT. IX.

IN exhibiting the practice of Pagan Virtue, we have perhaps somewhat exceeded the original, and borrowed some colouring from a diviner source; as the latter platonists, we are well aware, have adorned and improved philosophy with sublimer truths and more exalted moral documents, than were known to the ancient professors. It is in the school of Jesus alone, that we have the light of truth, and the perfection of virtue, without the art, or the studied eloquence of composition, to recommend the one or the other. Christian perfection is the highest human nature is at present capable of. It confers on man the truest grandeur,

deur, the moſt ſubſtantial wiſdom, and the ſincereſt happineſs. It may not, indeed, form the man into the ſpruce, the gay, the gaudy, the dreſſy, the dancing, the delicate, the ſmooth, the ſubtle and ſervile ſycophant; but it will give a ſimplicity and ſincerity to his words and actions, a dignity to his ſentiments, a complacency and candour to his manners, that humility and condeſcenſion, that ſweetneſs and benevolence of ſpirit, which the man of mode affects, but affects in vain to imitate. The ſincereſt chriſtian, paradoxical as it may ſeem, would perhaps be the beſt courtier in the world: honeſt, without views of intereſt; faithful and aſſiduous without ambition; ſincere without rudeneſs or inſult; compliant without art, and benevolent without deſign; faithful to his

SECTION IX.

his Prince, as to his GOD, and from the fame principle of duty and confcience;—the patron of virtue; a promoter of arts; a friend to his country, and to human kind;—not affecting the femblance, but practifing the fubftance of virtue;—at home and abroad, refpected and treated with honour, as always acting with honour, and good faith to others; prudent upon principle,. without craft; engaging without artifice; and condefcending without fervility; dauntlefs from no confcious guilt, and daring to the death, in the profecution of truth and duty.

Morality hath its ground-work in nature, and hath therefore been properly ftyled eternal and immutable. Revelation is a fuperftructure on the ground-work of nature, and confpi-

cuous

cuous for its superior strength, use, and beauty. The believer acts with more spirit and firmness, with more simplicity and sincerity, than the natural man; as informed by a clearer light, and influenced by more powerful motives and stronger convictions. If revelation hath enlarged the sphere of duty, it administers proportionable strength and aid in the performance. It speaks its divinity alike, by the virtues it exacts, and by the power it lends to their efficacy. Its graces are of a sublimer order, than any natural, artificial, or even moral qualities of the mere man. They are effects of the more immediate operation of GOD; they communicate with, they take firmer hold upon the soul, and diffuse themselves with more power and uniformity on the manners, and

external

external behaviour of the man. The believer thinks, and acts, with an eye to that prefence which nothing can deceive;—to a judgment which no art, or fecrefy, or fubterfuge, can evade or elude; and to an allotment of punifhments, or rewards, which nothing can exceed or equal. A confcioufnefs of his own unworthinefs, makes the believer modeft and humble.

The fenfe of a particular Providence, of the ever prefent GOD, with the profpect of a future and immortal ftate ;—a conviction that infinite rectitude, that fupreme love, orders and directs the whole univerfe of being; and that this infinite and all-gracious GOD, is your GOD, and your portion for ever, give the believer an acquiefcence, a ferenity, and complacency

placency of spirit, a benevolence in manner and expression, which no fashionable compliments, or artificial good breeding, can ever arrive at. A sincere believer will be believed; and is sure to gain the esteem, the trust, the confidence and love of all with whom he is connected. A believer as such cannot deceive you; or, should he be himself deceived, his mistake must have the happiest effect upon himself, and upon those he converses with; as it obliges him to whatever things are honest, are lovely, are of good report;—to forbearance, to forgiveness, to candour, to charity, and every act of beneficence toward the whole human race. The believer is what he seems; means what he says, and performs what he promises, or more. Acting, as he does, with a

strict

strict regard to truth and sincerity, he is not at liberty to practise any artificial policy, and dissimulation, in his commerce with mankind. Easy and happy in himself, from the principles of his faith, and the reflections of a good conscience, he wears the smile of peace upon his brow, and diffuses from the fulness of his heart, ease and happiness to all around him. His sublime views, his spiritual, his heavenly, his immortal hopes and expectations, raise him above the world, and exempt him from all the selfish, the sordid, and vexatious passions, which disquiet and disgrace life; give him a superior air, manner, and dignity, tempered with a humanity and complacency, which is not to be acquired at any court in Europe;—and our fine gentleman, accomplished and set

out

out with all the graces of France and Italy, when oppofed to one who has been educated in the fchool of Chrift, makes no better a figure than a monkey does when compared to a man. It is the morality of the Gofpel alone, which can raife man to that perfection which Lord Chefterfield would recommend to his fon: and a character formed upon the moral principles of the Gofpel (one of the ftrongeft proofs of its divinity) as much excels the mere man of fafhion, as the fubftance exceeds the fhadow, as truth furpaffes falfehood, or a real and fignal benefit conferred, does an infidious promife, or profeffion of beneficence.

HAD Lord Chefterfield read the Gofpel with the fame attention, with which he read Mr. *de Voltaire,* the
Cardinal

Cardinal *de Retz*, and Tacitus, he had not perhaps found the same brilliancy of language and pride of wit, which he admired in his favourite authors; but he had found heavenly graces dictated in all the simplicity of truth, operating by a divine energy, powerful to correct every obliquity, to eradicate every corruption, and to confirm and advance every kindlier and beneficent propensity in his nature: and his Lordship might have been, at the same time, the best christian, the most upright statesman, and the finest gentleman in the nation. We have only to lament, that a nobleman of such eminent abilities, should have been led by vanity, by nature, and the fashion of the world, to adopt and recommend principles subversive of public and private virtue, and of the strength,

strength, the security, the glory and happiness of his country.

If revelation would have this happy effect upon the morals and conduct of mankind, would it be less propitious to their interests and fortunes as men and citizens?

Let Britons say, if the happiness and glory of their constitution at home has been established, or their empire abroad extended, by policy without probity, by the artifice of sharpers, by the wantonness of wit, by the narrow views of selfish and mercenary spirits;—by men devoid of principles, morals, and religion;—by fribbles, by dancers, and debauchees;—by well-bred courtiers, and flattering sycophants;

SECTION IX.

cophants;—by expert dealers in small talk, and the chit-chat of the day?

Let Britons say, if the Graces alone have formed their councils, fought their battles, gained their victories, or advanced their conquests? Whether the strapping of the shoe, or the curling of the hair, have had any weight in the balance of Europe; or in any age or country, supplied the place of true wisdom, or martial virtue, in contributing to the growth and stability of empire?

War may ravage our country; plague, or famine, or pestilence, may thin our streets, and unpeople our villages, and in the end prove salutary, by purifying the moral world of its corruption, and forming us to a firmer and founder habit of virtue and piety. But more fatal than war, than famine and peſtilence, are principles of immorality and impiety, admired and adopted by the national taſte, and admitted into the national practice.— They prepare a people for exciſion rather than caſtigation; they unqualify them for the diſcharge of duty in peace or war; they diſſolve all the bonds of ſociety, and propagate a ſpirit of meanneſs and ſelfiſhneſs, of luxury and lewdneſs, of diſſimulation and treachery, of injuſtice and oppreſſion, and give free range to every ſenſual indulgence that may be faſhionable in the ſight of men, and not incur the cenſure of the laws.

Lord Chesterfield ſtands chargeable, in the eye of every competent judge

SECTION IX.

judge of propriety, with this spirit and these principles; and as such deserves our detestation, as one of the worst enemies to his country that Britain ever produced, a Mandeville not excepted: and were I at liberty to wish ill to my country, I could not wish it worse, than that its interests and affairs, at home and abroad, might be conducted by counsellors and heroes, by senators and statesmen, formed on the plan and principles of Lord Chesterfield.

But, this notwithstanding, these Letters have met with an uncommon degree of attention and applause from the world, have been, and are still read with much avidity and delight. Yet let me divert for a moment the candid reader's eye from the

SECTION IX.

page of Lord Chesterfield, while I ask him these few questions.

Do you find your heart bettered by the perusal? Are your morals improved? Are your passions restrained or conquered? Are the vices of nature corrected? Are the sorrows and troubles of life assuaged or softened; or the terrors of death smoothed and smiling with peace and comfort? Does the noble Lord give you so much as a philosophical grandeur of sentiment, by opening to your prospect the immensity of the present system, or the indefinite progression of the future? — Does his Lordship's knowledge of human nature shew you wherein its meanness, and wherein its greatness consists; — how to correct and raise the one, or to cultivate,

improve

improve and enlarge the other? Has the noble Lord explained or enforced the social, the moral, or religious duties; inflamed your love to your neighbour, your country or your GOD? Does nature adorned by his pencil wear a fairer hue? Or does virtue in his Lordship's drawing assume a more lovely form?

INSPIRED by his Lordship's public spirit, are you willing to bleed, to suffer or die for liberty, for virtue, and your country? Or do your hearts burn within you, while the British Peer, fired by the genius of ancient Greece and Rome, pours in upon you the spirit of patriotism in a torrent of eloquence and enthusiasm?

Do you find yourselves disposed by his Lordship's precepts to pay more reverence and regard to simplicity, sincerity and truth? Or are your breasts more open to the impulse of friendship, to cordial benevolence, and an undissembled love of mankind? Amidst the various speculations raised from his knowledge of human nature, do you find any calculated to remove your ignorance, to support your infirmities, to heal your sickness, to direct the wavering mind, and to still the throbbings of an aching heart? Do you feel your hearts more charmed, enflamed and elevated by the love of sacred wisdom displayed in the works of the noble writer? Do you observe his Lordship pointing out to you, amidst the vanities of this life, any real and moral good, any substantial, sublime and sovereign happiness? Or does our philosophic sage, from the

SECTION IX.

the experienced inanity of this *silly world*; direct your views to new and opening scenes, — to a variety of untried being, with a future manifestation of Godhead to display his perfections, and vindicate his present Providence?

SAY, Britons, is a life of dissimulation, of hypocrisy, of ceremony, of compliment, of flattery and servility; a life formed to the fashion of this world, devoted to passion, to pleasure, to selfishness and sensuality;— a life aspiring after nothing higher than the caresses of a mistress, or the friendship and favours of a court;— say, is this the life worthy of a being born with distinguished moral and intellectual powers, capable of pervading the works of GOD, of conceiving immortal

mortal hopes, and imitating the divine moral perfections?

Amidst our improvements and growing difcoveries in the natural, the moral and the intellectual fyftems;— amidft the fupernatural light of heaven, which hath difperfed the darknefs that obfcured the nations, are we to revert to the principles of Epicurus; are we to adopt chance or fortune for our GOD, and pleafure and paffion for our guides? Does the glory of man confift in imitating the beafts that perifh; in adopting their appetites, and wifhing and expecting to die their death? Is this the whole ambition of nobility?— To fhine the blazing meteors of a moment, and to confign their names, their effence and future profpects to corruption and forgetfulnefs?

SECTION IX.

getfulnefs? Are infamy in life, and the duft of death the only prerogatives, which man, as a reafonable being, was born to inherit? And what has the noble Lord propofed higher or greater for the object of your attainment or afpiration? What is the figure, and what the fortune he points out to his fon, but the reward of fervility and flattery, of venality and corruption? And if he affects to defy death, it is not from any rational hopes, conceived or expreffed, which might enable him to fupport or conquer it; but, like a vain bully, he affects the hero, in fighting an enemy whom he cannot efcape; and like a malefactor dragged to the place of execution, he dies hard, becaufe paft all hopes of a reprieve.

SAY,

SECTION IX.

SAY, Britons! Sons of reason, say, if amidst the awful revolutions, and births of time, and the majestic process of nature and providence; if, in the presence, and under the administration of an infinite and all-holy GOD, amidst the disappointments, the vanity, and misery of life, and under the certainty of dissolution and of death; say, if thus situated, you can think yourselves born merely for the song and dance — to indulge to passion and pleasure, to know nothing, to do and suffer nothing, to hope and possess nothing, but the short-lived good of the present moment? Say, is friendship and benevolence, is virtue, liberty, and your country, a mere name, or a nothing? Say, if your moral feelings, the natural operations of the soul, peace of conscience,
and

SECTION IX. 253

and the terrors of conscious guilt; if the sentiments of sages, of philosophers and legislators,—the deductions of reason, and the institutes of religion, are all nothing but a name? Say, if life and death, if time and eternity, if the apparatus of heaven and earth, if GOD, the judge of all, contain or imply nothing respecting you, but the momentary gratifications of your senses and passions, your vanity and vice? Away with this folly and madness — with these fond and childish conceptions and degenerate appetites! And let us, if not for GOD's sake, yet for our own, awake to the wants of nature, to the calls of providence, and to the voice of reason and religion: let us act, at least, the manly and philosophic part; and for the insipid, the gaudy, the superficial, the flimsy, and delicate

delicate creatures, which the Lord Chesterfield would make us, let us exert the conduct, and display the character of those who are called to be the sons of GOD and of glory.

WHAT is it then that charms you in the page of Lord Chesterfield? Acknowledge and blush, whilst you acknowledge it. It is his vanity stooping to, and corresponding with your vanity; his nobility condescending to be your caterer and pimp of pleasure; his easy and pliant virtue assuming any stamp, which the fashion of the world is pleased to impress upon it; flattering your passions, countenancing your follies, and indulgent to every corrupt propensity of your nature. You are charmed with his Lordship's private anecdotes, seasoned
with

with wit, with ribaldry, and scandal, tending to shade* some of the brightest names and characters that ever adorned, and to detract from the guilt and horror of some of the worst that ever disgraced human nature. You are charmed with a patriotism unembarrassed with integrity, conscience, and

---

* SOME circumstances he mentions in the Duke of Marlborough's youth, were certainly not intended to derive new honour upon the character of that illustrious general and distinguished statesman. All that he has to say of Brutus is, that he was a thief in Macedonia; he says not much better of Mr. Addison, whom we find him affectedly shy in mentioning, or recommending, amongst the English Classicks; and all that he has to tell us of this most ingenious, most elegant, most entertaining, and instructive writer is, that he stole his book of travels, or most of the remarks and classical references in that book, from Alberti, an old Italian author; and this the noble Lord gives us upon mere report or hearsay. Vol. III. p. 351.

love

love of country; and with a perfection devoid of morality and inward sanctity.

BRITONS, that are parents, afk your own hearts, fuppofing that Lord Chefterfield's fcheme of education was both poffible and practicable, and that you could reconcile the ardor of youth with the fagacity and cool diffimulation of old age:—that you could unite in the fame perfon, the two different characters of an Adonis and an Ulyffes, of a Paris and a Neftor, the wifdom and political fcience of a Walfingham, or a Burleigh, and the ambition and lewdnefs of a Somerfet, and a Buckingham:—Britons, who are parents, afk your own hearts, whether you would wifh your children to be educated on the Lord Chefterfield's plan?
Whether

SECTION IX.

Whether you would delight to fee them accomplifhed after his Lordfhip's idea of perfection? Making a figure and fortune in life at the expence of their innocence, their integrity, their fincerity, their liberty and independence? Would it pleafe you to fee them exchange the virtues for the graces? A good confcience for a plaufible appearance? Englifh honefty for French grimace? And found morals for external and fuperficial accomplifhments? Could you fincerely congratulate yourfelves, as having gained the grand point, when you beheld your fons, as mere courtiers, faithlefs politicians, prudent and polite debauchees, playing a fhort-lived part on the ftage of this filly world, then quitting it with an hardy indifference

rence what should become of them for ever?

Ye parents and sons of Britain, spurn the insidious tempter from your embrace: he offers an insult to your understanding, and the common sense of mankind. He builds your happiness on the ruins of your virtue: he recommends a course of conduct and manners, which disdains all connection with simplicity and truth — with the sincere love of GOD and man: he confines all your interest to this *silly world*, and employs your chief care in the cultivation of a frail and perishing body. The faculties of an aspiring and intellectual soul, with its proper objects, GOD and his works, his providence, perfections, and laws, he extinguishes or absorbs, in directing the whole man to the gratification

of

SECTION IX.

of the lufts of the flefh, the luft of the eye, and the pride of life. Men, and the Noble Lord among the reft, are only more refpectable animals, born to breathe, to live, to propagate, and rot; with wit only to difplay more vanity; and with reafon to practife more fraud and falfehood than their brother-brutes; but, in other refpects, the fame commoners of nature; living the fame life, and dying the fame death.

It is true, his Lordfhip does not affirm this in direct and exprefs terms, nor argue logically and fyftematically on the principles of religion and morality: but the moral lectures to his fon muft be confidered as fo many practical conclufions, derived from the principles of infidelity, taken for granted : and though the Noble Lord hath allowed, that the believer hath the advantage over the infidel in point of argument, yet he advifes, he moralizes, he concludes, as if divine truth and religious faith had no foundation or exiftence in reafon, or the nature of things: and the moft licentious of the infidel tribe have fcarce gone further, or fhewn more malice to mankind, than the Lord Chefterfield in his attempts to difcredit moral virtue, and to cancel all moral obligation.

THE genius of Britain is naturally ftrong and mafculine, great and enterprifing, ferious and thoughtful, difpofed to philofophy, to virtue, to opennefs, to integrity, to wifdom, to liberty and religion. None but an enemy to his country, or one ignorant

SECTION IX.

rant of its real interests, would wish to unbrace, and polish away this hardy and manly spirit, and to forego these native propensities and valuable privileges of our reasonable nature, for slavery, for sycophancy, and infidelity, for dissimulation and artifice, for vice, for falsehood and folly, for a compliment, a cringe, and a dance.

Upon the whole, what do these letters present us with, but the picture of a parent without true natural affection; of a man devoted to animal passions; of a wit without decency; of a moralist without virtue; of a senator without reverence to the laws; of a patrician without love to his country; of a statesman without integrity and public affection; of a practical infidel and epicurean; plausible rather than respectable; specious rather than virtuous; gracious than beneficent; complaisant not benevolent; easy not happy; gay and joyous, not serene or philosophical; vain and ostentatious, not great or elevated; a licentious wit, a wanton buffoon, not the dignified and sober statesman; studied in the frailties and imperfections, but unacquainted with the enlarged capacities and sublimer endowments of human nature;—a slave to sense and passion, but dead to the truth and comforts of the intellectual and spiritual world; alive to every vanity of life, but ignorant or insensible of the present GOD, and all immortal hope; eagerly grasping at feathers, at ribbons, at strings, at pebbles and shadows, but careless of the most important,

SECTION IX.

tant, of moral, of divine, of essential and eternal realities.

IF, after all, it be said in defence of Lord Chesterfield, that he wrote not for the public, and that as if ashamed of his principles or precepts he presumed or enjoined, that they should be preserved in inviolable secrecy, and that if he dealt in poison, it is only for his own and his son's use; this we acknowledge had been a sufficient excuse and the strongest argument for the non-publication of this collection; but now that they are sent into the world, and have all the influence and authority which the name, the character and example of Lord Chesterfield can give them, no apology need be made for any attempt to counterwork their mischievous effects and operations, and to awaken the world out of that delufive and immoral lethargy into which they are thrown by thefe fafcinating Letters.

If it fhould ftill be objected that we have ufed the noble Lord with too little ceremony, and have not paid him the refpect due to his title and quality, we reply that truth, virtue and religion, the interefts, the liberties and happinefs of mankind are great and momentous realities; in afferting which had we ufed a cautious referve, fervility, or flattery, we had avowed our fear of man, we had betrayed the caufe we profefs to defend, and had given encouragement to vice, by complimenting the vicious. A fycophant to the impious and immoral, whatever name or title they may bear, is a traitor to
his

SECTION IX.

his King, his Country, and his GOD. The virtues are what alone command our refpect, our homage and veneration. Lord Chefterfield, fuch as he appears in thefe Letters, has no claim to this veneration and refpect.

NEVER, perhaps, did there lefs real merit or fincere virtue appear, in any writer, than in his Lordfhip's genuine fentiments and advice to his fon. The fages, the legiflators, the philofophers, the patriots of the ancient pagan world were faints and heroes when compared with our Britifh moralift and patrician: whofe principles can be confidered in no other light, than as infamous to his name, baneful to his country, and degrading alike to his character as a man, a citizen, and a Briton.

SECTION IX.

Would any man be great indeed: let him facrifice his mean and fordid paffions, his vanity, and even his wit, to the ambition of being and doing the moft extenfive good to mankind. Let him be exalted above others more by his virtues, than by his ftation. Let him do honour to his fortune, his genius, and abilities, by the generous application of them to the relief of the needy, and the inftruction of the ignorant. Let his excellency appear by the folidity rather than by the luftre of his accomplifhments. If the great have not faculties of body or mind fuperior to thofe of other men, let them be content to rank with other men. Let them eftimate themfelves, as GOD and angels eftimate them; of an order, degree, and eminence which bear a juft proportion to their moral qualities,

their

www.ingramcontent.com/pod-product-compliance
Lightning Source LLC
Chambersburg PA
CBHW032102230426
43672CB00009B/1606